On My Mind – As the World Revolves

The Collected Essays of Martin Oliner
2015 – 2024

Copyright © 2024 by Martin Oliner

All rights reserved.

No portion of this book may be reproduced in any form without written permission from the publisher or author, except as permitted by U.S. copyright law.

Dedicated to Reva, my partner and love in life.

About the Author:

Martin Oliner was born in 1947 in a German DP camp. A child of Holocaust survivors, he was the first member of his family to graduate from high school and became a successful attorney, businessman, and self-made philanthropist.

Devoted to strengthening the ties between the United States and Israel, he currently serves as Co-President of the Religious Zionists of America-Mizrachi, Chair of Israel Bonds New York Region, Committee member of the Jewish Agency, Board member of B'nai B'rith, and a member of the United States Holocaust Memorial Council for a term expiring January 15, 2026.

Martin received a J.D. and an L.L.M. in Taxation with honors from New York University Law School, and is a member of Phi Betta Kappa and the Order of the Coif. He has taught at New York University Law School, Touro College School of Law, New York Law School and the School of Contemporary Studies at CUNY.

As an attorney, he has engaged in private practice since 1972 and has worked extensively with multinational financial institutions to restructure a wide variety of distressed investments in locations across the United States, Europe, and Asia.

Since 1992, Mr. Oliner has served full time as Chairman of the Board of Directors, President and Chief Executive Officer of First Lincoln Holdings, an insurance and real estate holding company. He has also served as a Director of Regency Equities, Asian Oceanic Capital Corporation, and New Navy LDA.

A passionate proponent of education, Martin served as one of six members of the Executive Board of Touro College and has been a trustee for over thirty years. In that time, he helped guide the College through significant, long term growth including the development of graduate and professional programs alongside an extensive building program with new campuses in Brooklyn, Queens, Manhattan, Long Island, Las Vegas and Los Angeles, a medical campus in Harlem, and new affiliated campuses in Moscow, Berlin and Israel.

He is also a founder of the San Francisco School of Osteopathic Medicine and has served as a director of the New York School of Podiatry.

He is the founding publisher and editor-in-chief of The Jewish Word, a monthly newspaper. His writings have been published extensively in the Jerusalem Post, The Jewish Press, and New York Jewish Week.

Locally, Martin was elected to the maximum three terms as the Mayor of the Village of Lawrence, New York where he served from 2010- 2016. He also served as President of his synagogue, Shaaray Tefila of Lawrence.

A resident of Lawrence, NY, Martin is married to Reva and they have three children and nine grandchildren.

Contact the author at: martinoliner@gmail.com or martinoliner@c4peace.org

Table of Contents

A letter to my grandson 1

Why vote for Torah? 5

Corker-Menendez: No bill is better than a bad bill 8

Defending against the lone wolf 12

Shabbat Shalom in Jerusalem 16

Trump not to blame for rise in antisemitism 19

An unbreakable alliance 23

A time for Jew-nity in Congress 26

Push for embassy move to Jerusalem with head held high 29

Jerusalem: the capital of Israel 32

Equivocating on Qatar 35

Skeptical of Saudi Arabia 37

The force to end terrorism 40

Recognizing all of Jerusalem, here to stay 43

Appreciating Israel's miracle at 70 with unity 45

Bringing Qatar into the fold 48

In praise of Trump's Passover cleaning 52

Looking ahead to Jerusalem's future 55

Showing appreciation for blessings from Trump 58

A religious Zionist's praise for Isaac Herzog 61

Response to a loving brother 63

The Jewish Nation-State Law outside politics 66

What GA delegates should learn from Jack Nagel 69

AIPAC must stay out of Israeli politics 72

Don't give up on the Democrats: The need for bipartisanship 75

AIPAC: Balancing bipartisanship and being thankful 78

Israel's election message to the world 81

On the blessings of bifurcation 84
If you will Trump's plan, it is no dream 87
25 years of Iran, Argentina, and terrorism 91
Give pressuring the Palestinians a chance 94
The double-edged sword of Omar and Tlaib 97
Why Tzom Gedalia's lesson of unity applies now 99
Israeli politicians and the sin of foolishness 102
A policy change of biblical proportions 105
Reaping rewards for remarkable courage 108
Trump's peace plan breaks new ground 112
US Jews must urge Israelis to safeguard the Trump-Netanyahu
relationship 115
Interview 118
Time for Israel, US to overcome COVID-19 and POLITICS-2020 120
Give Netanyahu his lasting legacy with annexation 123
UAE and Israel: A match made in heaven 127
Why Americans in Israel must vote for Trump 131
Voting for Trump as a multi-issue voter 134
WZO victory achieved through 'wall-to-wall' coalition 138
Take your time in dismissing Donald Trump 141
Not enough done to stymie scourge of antisemitism 144
Naftali Bennett lied his way to the top 147
Jews need to be united on a united Jerusalem 150
Ensuring the Abraham Accords 153
Diaspora Jews should at least be let into Israel 156
Netanyahu, sign the plea deal to help save the world 159
Ruth Calderon is unfit to head the Jewish Agency 161
It's wrong to eulogize World Mizrachi 164
Iranian attack on US should wake up Israel 168

Israel must say 'no' to Tom Friedman 171
Israel today pilfering from the public for pluralism 174
Why religious Zionists should vote for Smotrich.................................. 178
Netanyahu needs to choose Smotrich over Biden 182
Jewish American organizations endorsing antisemitism must be denounced.. 185
Netanyahu's Israeli gov't must stop coddling Qatar 188
Are the Abraham Accords proving to be a success? 191
Interview.. 194
How not to make peace between Israel and Saudi Arabia 197
Will Israel, Jewish world be less polarized in the Jewish New Year? ..202
What is Israel's endgame in Gaza? 205
10 Lessons for a Better 2024 211
Interview: 'We are paying the price for twenty years of neglect'.......... 216
Antisemitism is only getting worse across the world, including in Israel 218
When Schumer became his brothers' reaper 223
Following Iran's attack, more US aid is needed for Israel.................... 228
Still trust Biden on Israel? Don't... 231
When diplomacy fails: It's time for Israel to bomb and invade Lebanon 235
A great existential threat: A Harris presidency's impact on Israel 239
How Pro-Israel Americans Could Keep Kamala From Becoming President 243
How Israelis Could Keep Kamala From Killing Them 247
Index 251

A letter to my grandson

An Iggeres for the new generation

Dear Shimon Yedidya,

It has been more than 750 years since the Ramban wrote a letter in Akko in Eretz Yisrael and sent it to his son in Catalonia, Spain.

The letter has withstood the test of time, and it is still read around the world on a weekly basis, as the Ramban requested of his son. I make a point of reading it every week to inspire me to be humble and to appreciate that everything in life comes from Hashem.

There are those who would say that humility is no longer a respected attribute in a generation when people constantly glorify themselves on social media. But I beg to differ.

In a global world, in which people are more connected than ever, we must strive to be more modest than ever. When much of the world has been turned upside down, it is our duty as Jews to fix the world and make it better.

You live in a world that is broken in ways the Ramban could not have imagined. But you must see this as an opportunity, because it means that there is more that you can do to perfect not only your surroundings but the entire planet.

Unlike the Ramban's son, who could only live in one place at a time, your ability to reach out around the world is infinite. Your influence is not limited by space, though it is limited by time, which as you get older you will realize is truly the world's scarcest natural resource.

The sanctity of time is one of the themes of Parshas Behar-Bechukosai that you will be layning at your bar mitzvah. It describes how even land needs both a time for work and a time for rest, just like we do.

The parsha speaks of blessings and of curses. Having lived through a pandemic, you understand what it is like to live in both at much too early an age. You have seen how effective leadership is essential in times of crisis but that there are times when mankind is helpless and can only rely on the blessings of God.

"In all your actions, words and thoughts, always regard yourself as standing before Hashem, with His Shechinah above you, for His glory fills the whole world," the Ramban wrote his son.

When he wrote that, it was probably hard to comprehend how to constantly feel God's presence. Nowadays, when cell phone cameras are so ubiquitous, everyone knows they are constantly being watched.

That means we must always be on our best behavior. We must strive to be role models, not just to our younger siblings but to other Jews of all ages and to the gentiles around the world who are anything but indifferent about the future of the Jewish people.

"Examine your actions every morning and evening," the Ramban recommended.

There is no better time to start doing that than your bar mitzvah. Until that day, all your sins go to your parents, but from then on, they are yours alone.

We must constantly consider how to become better people, learning from our mistakes and our faulty judgment along the way.

It is the ability to capitalize on trial and error that has made the Jewish State of Israel so effective and successful. It happens in the IDF, in hi-tech and lessons are even eventually learned in politics.

You are fortunate to live in an era when travelling between Israel and the Diaspora has never been easier. The difficulties in air travel during COVID-19 were a reminder of how much we should appreciate how easy it is to get around when there is no pandemic.

Israel showed the world its blessings during the COVID crisis. The little Jewish state vaccinated its people faster than any country around the world, in part because its health system was the most organized. The curses of the coronavirus did not spare Israel, of course, but it did unite its people.

Israel remains a beacon of freedom and democracy and a safe harbor for all Jews, which the Holocaust taught us is a necessity and not a privilege.

The land and State of Israel are gifts that were a reality when you were born, but you cannot take them for granted. Many children only several years older than you lost their lives fighting to ensure that you could come to Israel and live a life of blessings in your biblical homeland.

Israel remains a work in progress, and you have the tremendous opportunity to take part in perfecting it. We religious Zionists see this as an opportunity to partner with Hashem in a mitzvah that generations of Jews could only pray for. It was the Ramban who first taught the world about the importance of living in Israel as a mitzvah.

Perhaps the hardest requests the Ramban made of his son were to study Torah well and to focus when he prays. These tasks have become more challenging in a world full of distractions.

But they are the duty of a Jew, who must constantly be learning and who has the honor of communicating with God three times a day. Spend your spare time reading and not being disturbed.

The more we learn, the more we realize we still do not know and how far we still have to go in our education. Never pretend you know all the answers.

"I don't know" is often the wisest response and of course, the most honest.

It is also the most humble answer, and people will appreciate that.

There are way too many know-it-alls nowadays. The world suffers from a shortage of the humble.

Perhaps reading this once a week can help start changing that. But the world is full of people who can give better advice than I can.

Your name, Shimon Yedidya, means that you are both a listener and a friend of God. Those are two wonderful things to be. Continue to live up to your name.

As the Ramban concluded to his son, I leave you with hope that you will "succeed and merit the World to Come which lies hidden away for the righteous."

Love,
Zayde

The Jewish Press

Why vote for Torah?

APRIL 26, 2015

In the current climate, it is almost impossible to enter an Orthodox synagogue in America that has not undertaken security measures on behalf of the institution. Time, money, and efforts of all types are expended. Members are passionately recruited to protect and ensure the physical welfare and safety of congregants and members.

Yet, even as Orthodox Jews throughout the nation firmly adhere to the mantra, "If you see something, say something," they have, until recently, been blind to, and silent about, a different type of threat. This is a spiritual threat from within that is arguably as insidious and challenging to Orthodox Jewish survival as any physical threat.

In October 2015, the 37th World Zionist Congress (WZC), the "parliament" of the Jewish people, will convene in Israel. At that time, the slate of leaders and policy stewards of the World Zionist Organization (WZO) that the Jewish people had voted for before April 30th, will assume their mantle of leadership. The WZO and its constituent and affiliate organizations are empowered to distribute more than one billion dollars to support programs throughout Israel and the Diaspora.

Vying for dominance in this election, are movements within our nation which seek to undermine and subvert Orthodox Judaism. These groups are using the WZC election to facilitate that attack.

These other streams are attempting to first hijack and usurp the financial resources that fuel Orthodox educational programs and materials. They are seeking to subvert the funding of the Hesder yeshivot, the subsidization and financing of services to Orthodox communities in Israel, and the grants and funding of Orthodox Shlichim and emissaries that are so effective in so many schools and institutions throughout America.

With an agenda far beyond merely derailing Orthodoxy financially, these streams also seek to undermine the ideals, convictions and beliefs that are the life-blood of Torah-committed Jews and which these programs both sustain and perpetuate.

The unabashedly stated goals of these other streams are diametrically opposed to fundamental Orthodox religious values, which include Religious Zionist outreach, Torah inspired education, the sanctity of a united Yerushalayim, intra-marriage, and advancing Aliyah. They decry the idea of halachically performed conversions and the preservation of Shabbat in Israel. Undermining all of this and more are the stated positions and goals of the other streams.

Shockingly, many of their positions are not only anathema to those who are Torah-motivated, but create an existential danger to the Jewish State itself.

How so?

Some of the pronouncements of these streams include the advocacy of the nascent and growing BDS movement – "Boycott, Divestiture and Sanctions." They view support of BDS as necessary "tough love" – as they view other criticisms of Israel, the support and validation of intermarriage, and the undermining of Yehuda and Shomron.

It is imperative that Orthodox supporters of Israel recognize the current challenge. This is no mere theoretical point. It is not just another academic debate between theologians or a mere battle over funding.

It is an existential threat to Orthodoxy.

It is a threat driven by a blind selfish refusal to admit that, following the Pew Reports highlighting of Orthodox Judaism's viability and vitality, it appears that adherence to a Torah way of life holds the key to Jewish survival.

In contrast to the war being waged against them, the Orthodox community is not seeking to dominate nor aggressively confront any other stream nor to be proselytizing. It is simply striving to preserve its own priorities and fundamental Orthodox religious beliefs. The Orthodox community is attempting to make clear, through successful presentation in the WZC election, that it is the presumptive voice of the Jewish people on the world stage.

Thanks to Divine assistance rendered to whatever efforts and resources we have been able to marshal, the Jewish people have survived and overcome physical threats from without for millennia. It is the threat from within, the threat we often choose neither to see nor to say something about, that has too often been our misfortune. Such a threat has arisen again.

Before April 30th, every Orthodox Jew must see, register, and vote for VOTE TORAH – The Religious Zionist Slate, so that our people, our Torah, our Nation endure.

The Jerusalem Post

Corker-Menendez: No bill is better than a bad bill

MAY 13, 2015

Iron pyrite is a mineral with a metallic luster that resembles gold. Also known as fool's gold, it is actually not related to gold at all. The currently pending Corker-Menendez bill ("the bill"), designed to give Congress some control over the impending Iran deal ("the deal"), displays a remarkable resemblance to iron pyrite.

At first blush, it seems to be just the type of statute needed to allow Congress to weigh in on the deal. If the deal proves to be disastrous, Congress can nix it. What better arrangement could there be? The bill, also known as the Iran Nuclear Agreement Act of 2015, was co-sponsored by a bipartisan team – Senate Foreign Relations Committee Chairman Bob Corker (R-Tennessee) and former ranking minority member Sen. Bob Menendez (D-New Jersey).

The goal of it was to prevent a bad deal and to provide a web of delays, a few stops, and a poison pill in order to shore up Congress's ability to review the deal.

Closer examination, however, shows that the bill is just as illusory as iron pyrite.

Here's why: The bill does not do what it should – namely require, in this specific instance, that Congress vote to approve any agreement between Iran and President Barack Obama before it goes into effect, as the Constitution requires for any treaty between the United States and another nation. This bill, essentially, does the reverse. It allows the deal to take effect immediately, unless and until Congress votes to disapprove of it.

Here is an analogy. In the state of Kansas, a 12-year-old girl can get married with the consent of her parents. In general, it may not be a good idea for a 12-year-old girl to get married, but perhaps with the parents' prior approval, it may be workable. Now imagine if the Kansas marriage law was rewritten to allow any 12-year-old girl to get married on her own, with the sole caveat that six months later her parents could disapprove of the marriage and dissolve it.

Such an arrangement would not be a good idea – neither for the 12-year-old girl nor for the United States – and this is but the first problem with Corker-Menendez.

The second problem is that the bill hands over to the president a newly-contrived path that only serves to help him elevate the status of his Iran deal. It has essentially created a legislative device that lies somewhere between the treaties referred to in our Constitution and a naked executive agreement.

The Constitution states that the president has the right to initiate treaties that commit the United States, but that those treaties are not effective until ratified by a two-thirds vote of the Senate. Precisely because of this limitation, presidents who wish to circumvent Congress avoid the word "treaty" and try to utilize different avenues to achieve their objectives.

In order to implement policy without Congressional input, presidents can make use of what is called an "executive agreement."

These agreements can be negotiated in a manner that sidesteps Congress, allowing presidents to handle foreign policy by themselves and avoid the "treaty" process mandated by the Constitution.

Executive agreements have limitations.

They can be rescinded by a future president.

The Corker-Menendez bill creates a Congressionally- blessed executive agreement. It has the advantages of a near-treaty because Congress has in essence signed off on a path for the deal. It will now be much more difficult for the next president to undo this executive agreement.

The president needs this bill to give his executive agreement more pizazz and lift, but Congress had other alternatives. Under this "super-charged" executive agreement, Congress has simultaneously blessed the deal now and has muzzled itself for the future. This self-muzzling of Congress is on two fronts. Firstly, the ability to stop sanctions relief and slow down the dismantling of it is going to be much more difficult for Congress to achieve. Secondly, the ability of Congress to add additional sanctions will be severely hampered.

Losing Congress's voice of dissent by passing the Corker-Menendez bill is neither in the national interest nor in Israel's interest, notwithstanding AIPAC's current position supporting the bill.

Those advocating for the bill argue that it is a necessary compromise because the president would have vetoed any other legislation requiring prior approval of a deal and that they in turn did not have the 2/3 votes of Congress that are needed to override that veto.

This assumption of a veto is unclear because there are advantages to the president to have any Congressionally blessed executive agreement. However, what is certain is that under Corker, those who are unsatisfied with the deal will have no recourse. Once the deal is signed, an unsatisfied Congress would by joint resolution disapprove, but the president who entered into the deal would veto that resolution.

Clearly, such a veto would be more sustainable by the president after the deal is signed than against a bill which required prior Congressional approval.

Furthermore, now more than ever an information campaign must be launched to educate the public as to how disastrous it would be to have yet another North Korea.

When a country still views the United States as the Great Satan and has a rallying cry of "Death to the USA"; when it arms terrorist movements to destabilize governments and murder innocents; when it actually succeeds in destabilizing governments – it cannot be allowed to emerge as a regional power replete with nuclear weapons – even if it may be a counterforce to an emerging and ever-growing Islamic State.

Corker-Menendez is a device that provides political cover for Democrats who do not wish to confront the president because the bill, in the final analysis, requires a two thirds vote of Congress to disapprove the deal in order for the deal to be rejected. In the interim, it silences Congress's voice of dissent and thereby places any would-be campaign against the deal in a veritable strait-jacket.

Corker-Mendendez must be rejected. No bill is better than a bad bill.

The Jewish Press

Defending against the lone wolf

MARCH 7, 2016

Since its founding, and even before, the State of Israel has repeatedly called upon its civilian population to assist in addressing and repelling any threat to its security and existence. Thus, at its inception, when challenged by conventional, nation-led military forces, Israelis served in their citizen army. Thereafter, in response to constant threat and sporadic attack, Israelis remained, and continue to remain, on "reserve," notwithstanding the myriad sacrifices such service entails.

When assaulted from rockets above, Israeli civilians assisted the government in their own protection by taking to bomb shelters. When threatened by the possibility of chemical warfare, Israelis donned gas masks. In their own defense, as well as the defense of their neighbors and nation, the Israeli populace has always been prepared to step forward and respond as the situation requires.

The current "knife intifada" has, since September, resulted in the murder of 30 innocent Israelis as well as injury to another 352. The Ministry of Foreign Affairs reports 179 stabbings and attempted stabbings, 38 vehicular ramming attacks, and 74 shootings.

The "knife intifada" represents a new terror stratagem, one that focuses almost entirely on "lone wolves," who forego large casualty attacks for isolated acts of violence that not only kill, maim, and spread fear and paralysis within communities, but are almost immune to both intelligence gathering efforts and effective preventive action.

Thus, argues security expert as well as former MK and member of the Knesset Foreign Affairs and Defense Committee, Yoni Chetboun, the current paradigms for confronting terrorism are "no longer relevant in the face of the Intifada of the knives" and to "defeat it, Israel's basic security doctrine must undergo a radical shift."

That shift, according to Chetboun and many others, is to tap into "the Israeli fighting spirit to facilitate a grassroots counter-mobilization of citizens to protect their own communities," and institute, beyond the still-necessary conventional military and counter-terrorism tactics, a new, third level of civilian defense. This added component to Israel's anti-terrorist strategy would include the infusion of armed civilians in the anti-terrorist effort.

Proponents of enlisting licensed firearm owners to be on-site first responders, note numerous incidents where quick thinking and adequately armed civilians prevented further carnage by eliminating terrorists before security forces could arrive or even be notified. Supporters of increasing the number of armed civilians, readily available to step in and engage spontaneous attack include many police chiefs, the Mayor of Jerusalem, Public Security Minister Gilad Erdan, and the Knesset Caucus on Firearms Policy led by Likud MK Amir Ohana.

Plans include allowing licensed gun owners to carry their side-arms with them at all times and easing the current restriction on gun ownership, which is deemed onerous by many. Unlike the United States where the Second Amendment cites the "right" to bear arms, in Israel owning a weapon is not deemed a right but rather an intensely regulated privilege. As a result, despite the obvious threat to its citizenry, there are only 7.3 legal civilian-owned handguns per 100 Israelis. Currently those seeking a gun permit must be trained, pass a rigorous investigation, can only purchase a weapon from a licensed gun shop, be of a certain age, present a medical note and a specific reason for the request, and agree to be limited to owning only one firearm and an unreplenishable lifetime supply of only fifty bullets.

Under MK Ohana's plan, those allowed to obtain a gun license would now include anyone without a problematic criminal or mental health record, who has attended an annual session at a shooting range, and who performs reserve duty. Given that there are 445,000 reservists, this plan could increase the number of legally-owned civilian handguns within the State of Israel by almost two-thirds, thereby enhancing Israel's internal security dramatically.

Opponents of relaxed gun-licensing fear an increase in domestic violence incidents, random homicides, and vigilantism. Adding to the debate (albeit, in the opinion of many, not relevant to the debate) was the comment by the Israel Defense Forces Chief of Staff, while discussing the army's rules of engagement, that he "would not want to see a soldier empty a magazine [to shoot] a young girl with scissors."

Although the comment was seen by some as a criticism of using deadly physical force to combat terrorists, the army, officials, and even Prime Minister Netanyahu saw the comment as a reaffirmation of Israel's moral commitment to combat terrorism using the minimum required power while still asserting that the use of whatever power is required to meet any given threat, remains imperative and appropriate. Meanwhile, in the interim, the IDF, following the murder of an IDF sergeant killed fighting off terrorists bare-handed, has ordered soldiers to bring their weapons home with them.

Advocates of more armed civilians insist that those so empowered would coordinate, as in Judea and Samaria, with governmental security services and would eventually be augmented by mobile apps to alert authorities. Nor does anyone suggest this added line of self-defense would result in "shoot first, and ask questions later" scenarios because the current situation of knives being plunged into innocent, randomly targeted individuals unambiguously and unquestionably justifies and demands immediate action with no questions needed at all.

Beyond responding directly to, and in fact removing, specific "lone wolves," increasing the number of on-any-site-and-every-site armed civilians would result in a communal feeling of security. More so than even the actual physical result, crucial as that is, there would be the ensuing confidence of a community in control of its environs and protective of, as well as by, its own residents. It is an initiative that not only fights terrorists, but terrorism itself.

The people of Israel have always placed their faith in their G-d, their government, and themselves. Thrust upon them now by an ever-resourceful and demented enemy is the need to continue that faith as before, but to augment it by reliance on not just isolated heroes, but on a nation of civilian heroes ready, willing, and most importantly, able to protect themselves and each other.

The Jewish Press

Shabbat Shalom in Jerusalem

JUNE 23, 2016

Cities are visited and lived in because one wants to do business there, eat there, tour there, study there or celebrate there.

There is one city, however, that, while it offers all of the above, recognizes that it is unique to history because people simply want to be there; that for centuries visitors and residents have reveled in the pure joy of being there and nowhere else; to simply walk its streets and absorb the intangible, whether it be its spirit, its pain, its glory, and, most of all, its holiness, the amorphous, indescribable connection to heaven and G-d.

That city is Jerusalem, deemed by our sages to be two cities: one planted forever on earth to serve as the world's spiritual center, inextricably bound to a second Jerusalem, one on-high where departed souls and celestial beings reflect the purity and sanctity of that second Jerusalem onto the one below. Indeed, one can argue that it is that continuum, that eternal flow that accounts for the inexplicable satisfaction of just being in Jerusalem and our survival as a nation.

Over the years, during my many visits to Yerushalayim, I have come to realize that the inarticulable but genuine euphoria felt by one's physical presence in Jerusalem finds expression in the universal greeting of "Shabbat Shalom" and the smile that inevitably accompanies it.

Somehow, wishing another the blessing of Sabbath peace from on-high, while offering the very real human gifts of joy and friendship as reflected in a smile, combines the essence of Jerusalem, and what makes it so special. "Shabbat Shalom and a smile" are a statement and a gesture enhanced, enriched and made holy because of where spoken and made, a statement and a gesture that, for me, define the city.

Yet, of late, as I stroll through Yerushalayim, I can't help but notice the increasing absence of both the statement and the gesture, as all too often neither is offered nor returned. For all too many just "being" in Jerusalem is not enough, as a city that blends heaven and earth is deemed by them just another city that induces neither blessing nor smile.

This past week my wife, Reva, and I attended the middle school graduations of our granddaughter, Olivia (Simona), and our grandson, Ethan (Ozer Shimon), who was asked to recite the Prayer for Israel and Peace. Prior to doing so, he recounted his reaction to his younger brother, Calvin's (Shalom's) bar mitzvah, celebrated several days earlier in Jerusalem.

To my great joy, he noted that while he appreciated every aspect of the event as well as the spirit and sacrifice of the Israeli people and IDF, for him there were two great highlights: One, was his realization that the event, attended by all his uncles, aunts and cousins from both the Friedman and Oliner families who came for the Shavuos weekend to hear his brother lain at both the Kotel and Great Synagogue, confirmed our oft-repeated statements about the value and beauty of family. His remarks reflected my own comment at the simcha that, while all else is transient and fleeting, the bond of family endures; that, while as my mother, z"l, (his great grandmother and a Holocaust survivor) observed: "everything can be taken from you except that which is within you," that which is within you that is truly meaningful, is placed there by family, teachers, rebbeim and study.

His other highlight was the fact that so many Israelis shared his family's joy: from the cab driver who threw candies and sang Mazel Tov to the restaurateurs who treated our simcha as their own. We are one great family and nation.

As he spoke, I suddenly remembered that on the Shabbos of the bar mitzvah as our entire family walked the streets of Jerusalem, talking, laughing, exchanging ideas and thoughts, happy to be a family reveling in Calvin's beautiful laining on Shabbos and Shavuos and, as one, happy to just be in Yerushalayim, everyone we encountered greeted us with a "Shabbat Shalom" and a smile. It was, indeed, Shalom's Shabbat.

The Yiddish word for grandchildren "ainiklech" is said to be derived from the Biblical verse "and the burning bush was not consumed" (ainennu ukol).

One can only trust and believe that those in Yerushalayim Shel Maala, seeing grandchildren (and great grandchildren) happy to be in Jerusalem and appreciating its holiness will ensure that G-d will bless and guard us, and that the burning bush will never be consumed.

The Jerusalem Post

Trump not to blame for rise in antisemitism

It can be argued that antisemites perceived Obama's policies as supportive of their own views.

APRIL 5, 2017

President Donald Trump's critics were quick to blame him for an apparent rise in antisemitic incidents in the United States.

The folly of those critics was exposed with last month's arrest of a 19-year-old American Israeli, who has been accused of perpetuating the overwhelming majority of some 150 bomb threats to Jewish organizations across the US in the first months of 2017.
Removing those bomb threats from the list of antisemitic incidents could demonstrate that, despite all the reports about rising antisemitism since Trump took office, the number of antisemitic incidents is actually down.

During the administration of president Barack Obama, more than 7,000 antisemitic attacks occurred but did not make waves in the media. At that time, no one thought to blame Obama for the antisemitic incidents in the manner in which Trump is currently being blamed.
A case can be made that the antisemitic incidents since Obama left office can be attributed not to the rise of Trump, but to Obama's departure.

During Obama's term in office, his efforts to challenge the Jewish state were always in the headlines.

Anti-semites in America could keep their hatred for Jews beneath the surface because, from their perspective, an anti-Israel (and thus anti-Jewish) position was already being implemented at the highest level.

It should be acknowledged that Obama has always spoken very warmly about the American Jewish community, with whom he has had close ties since his days as a community organizer in Chicago in the 1980s. Indeed, his hagiographer, Atlantic magazine editor-in-chief Jeffrey Goldberg, even called him "the first Jewish president."

President Obama also provided Israel with unprecedented, guaranteed military aid that cannot be included in Trump's planned foreign aid cutbacks. It was the most generous financial package ever offered to Israel by any US president.

Yet, since Israel's founding, the Jewish state has been a channel for articulating and implementing antisemitism. As Defense Minister Avigdor Liberman claims, it is not Israel's policies but its very existence that generates antisemitism. One can add to that envy of the Jewish state's extraordinary success, which was once again recently demonstrated by the sale of Jerusalem-based Mobileye to Intel for $15 billion.

It can be argued that antisemites perceived Obama's policies as supportive of their own views. In his June 4, 2009 speech at Cairo University, Obama undermined Israel's narrative of the Jewish state's continuous existence because of its connection to its land going back to the biblical patriarchs and matriarchs. He adopted the false Palestinian narrative that Israel exists only because of the Holocaust.

Obama further reinforced that false narrative by going straight from Cairo to the Buchenwald concentration camp and not to Jerusalem.

Obama also encouraged the development of J Street, an organization that has actively polarized the Jewish community and made Israel into a divisive issue instead of the unifying force it has heretofore been on Capitol Hill. The president tried (and failed) to do the same with Israelis, urging dovish college students in Jerusalem to push their political leaders to take risks on behalf of peace.

The tensions between Obama and Prime Minister Benjamin Netanyahu were initiated by Obama to demonstrate to the Arab world that the US was no longer "in Israel's pocket."

Former Obama adviser Dennis Ross wrote in his book Doomed to Succeed: The US-Israel Relationship from Truman to Obama that

Obama made a deliberate, strategic decision to add daylight between the US and Israel to improve his relations with the Muslim world.

Obama also made a strategic decision to seek a deal with Iran, the terrorism- supporting Islamic republic that sponsors contests for antisemitic cartoons.

But one could argue that perhaps no action by Obama encouraged antisemitism more than his efforts over his eight years in office to demonize Israeli settlements. Those efforts sometimes subtly, sometimes overtly portrayed Israel as an aggressor, and incorrectly painted the Jewish state as the primary obstacle to Middle East peace and the sole source of Palestinian misery.

That effort culminated in December with the refusal of the Obama administration to veto UN Security Council Resolution 2334, which states that the establishment by Israel of settlements in the Palestinian territory including east Jerusalem, "occupied" since 1967, has no validity, constitutes a flagrant violation of international law and is a major obstacle to the achievement of the two-state solution and a just, lasting and comprehensive peace.

The resolution demands that Israel immediately and completely cease all settlement activities in the "occupied territories," including east Jerusalem.

It implicitly encouraged the International Criminal Court to prosecute Israeli officials as war criminals for advancing West Bank construction.

The most harmful impact of the resolution is the provision that "Calls upon all states to distinguish, in their relevant details, between the area of the State of Israel and the territories occupied since 1967."

It is noteworthy that this provision contravenes existing American state and federal legislation. The Boycott, Divest, and Sanctions (BDS) movement is a decade-old international campaign, modeled after the South Africa divestment campaign, to place crippling economic pressure on the State of Israel until it submits to conditions supportive of the Palestinians.

In recent years, BDS has been successfully combated by state and federal legislation. Such legislation makes the rejection of BDS a top priority for US negotiators as they work on free trade agreements. Yet, when he signed the anti-BDS Trade Facilitation and Enforcement Act in February 2016, president Obama said he would not enforce it with regard to Israeli settlements.

With such a friend as Barack Obama in the White House, the Jewish People's enemies did not feel compelled to act. Now with Donald Trump, a president perceived as truly pro-Israel, they have resurfaced to ensure that antisemitism will continue, not because of the policies of the White House.

The Jewish Press

An unbreakable alliance

MAY 12, 2017

In the 50 years since the 1967 Six Day-War, Israel has grown into a technological, economic, and military regional superpower in the Middle East.

A nearly nonexistent inflation rate and low unemployment have helped propel Israel to third in the world after Hong Kong and South Korea on a list of the world's most stable and promising economies for 2016 published by the Bloomberg financial news agency.

According to the World Happiness Report published in March by the UN Sustainable Development Solutions Network and the Earth Institute at Columbia University, Israel is the 11th-happiest country in the world for the fourth year running.

Israel fared better than the United States in both of those studies, prompting questions about where the quality of life is better these days.

Nevertheless, Israel still needs America, now more than ever. And Israel is an ally America can count on in the volatile Middle East.

The U.S.-Israel alliance endured despite the poor personal relations between Obama and Israeli prime minister Benjamin Netanyahu. Former Obama adviser Dennis Ross wrote in his book Doomed to Succeed: The US-Israel Relationship from Truman to Obama that Obama made a strategic decision to put daylight between the U.S. and Israel in order to improve U.S. relations with the Muslim world.

But by the end of his tenure, Obama had upgraded annual military aid for Israel from $3.1 to $3.8 billion.

There were Israelis who called for rejecting American military aid and turning elsewhere. After all, Israel fared well in the Six-Day War before the U.S. started aiding the IDF and before the Yom Kippur War reminded Israelis of their vulnerability. But those calls were rejected by Netanyahu, who made a deal with Obama despite his hopes that whoever won the American election would be better for Israel.

For Israel, America acts as a strategic buffer between the Jewish state and hostile world and – as has been repeatedly proven – the only friend that it can truly count on in good times and bad.

When the international community received indications from the White House that positive treatment of Israel was not a prerequisite for good ties in Washington, Israel suffered accordingly.

Now, under President Trump, more and more world leaders have realized that the road to Washington once again passes through Jerusalem. Israeli media have reported that many diplomats in Washington have turned to Israel's ambassador Ron Dermer for help getting to Trump advisers Jared Kushner and Steve Bannon.

The perception of close ties between Netanyahu and Trump have helped Netanyahu improve his relations with Europe and Asia. Netanyahu has not been afraid to dictate new terms to Europe, vowing not to meet with visiting European leaders who meet with representatives of Israeli NGOs perceived by him as demonizing Israel and its military.

During this renaissance in Israel's relations with the U.S., Netanyahu is working behind the scenes to prevent the potential existential threat of the nuclearization of Iran. Looking to the future, Netanyahu is working with Trump to ensure the Islamic Republic will not emerge from the Syrian civil war with a foothold on the Mediterranean and on the border with Israel.

Meanwhile, solid ties are being maintained with top Democrats in the Senate and House of Representatives, sustaining the bipartisan relationship that is such a vital asset for Israel, a small country struggling with constant threats from terror, anti-Semitism, boycotts, and the divestment and sanctions movement.

On May 17, 25 national Jewish organizations will gather at the Capitol with Congressional leadership from both houses and parties to initiate a resolution commemorating the 50th anniversary of the reunification of Jerusalem.

With Congress rarely agreeing on anything these days, it is no small accomplishment to bring this group together for this commemoration.

The event is proof that just as the alliance with the United States unites the very divided people of Israel, the Jewish state brings the very divided American leadership together, at a time when a strong U.S.-Israel relationship is more critical than ever for both countries.

The Jerusalem Post

A time for Jew-nity in Congress

This is our opportunity to wipe out the ignominy that has been with us since 1948. Our goal is clear: to wipe Israel off the map.

MAY 13, 2017

Fifty years ago, the people of Israel and Jews around the world came together – in fear.

War was imminent between Israel and its Arab neighbors. There were legitimate worries that the Jewish state would be annihilated.

On the Syrian front alone Israel was vastly outnumbered, with just a handful of tanks – all that were available because Israel had not yet built a security alliance with the United States.

Egyptian leader Gamal Nasser told Egyptian National Assembly Members that the time had come to restore the Middle East to how it was before Israel was formed in 1948.

"The existence of Israel is an error which must be rectified," echoed Iraqi president Abdur Rahman Aref. "This is our opportunity to wipe out the ignominy that has been with us since 1948. Our goal is clear: to wipe Israel off the map."

In response to this existential threat, a national unity government was formed in Israel, with opposition leader Menachem Begin joining the governing coalition for the first time and revered former general Moshe Dayan becoming defense minister.

Not only did Israel win an impressive victory over Egypt and Syria, after Jordanian king Hussein ignored Israel's pleas to stay out of the war, the IDF won control over the Old City of Jerusalem and its holy sites.

For 19 years prior to that, Jerusalemites could only peer into the Old City from the nearby YMCA. Jerusalem was full of barbed wire. Touching the Western Wall and other holy sites was a dream for them. It was as if Israel's War of Independence in 1948 had not yet been completed until 1967.

As the president of the Religious Zionists of America, I wholeheartedly believe that the IDF's victory over so many Arab armies in just six days was a great miracle. I also believe that human beings must make an effort to partner with God in bringing His miracles to fruition.

Israel has paid the painful price of defending its country, losing some 25,000 of its best and brightest to war and terrorist attacks. Israel owes its continued existence to those soldiers and civilians who have enabled the miracle of a Jewish state.

The leaders of Israel have also done their part in guiding the country to security and working on achieving peace. Repairing internal divides has proven just as challenging for Israel, which has absorbed immigrants from around the world with a myriad of ethnic, religious and political divides.

Israel's ability to become unified in times of great distress against all odds is part of the secret of its success. Similarly, those of us who head Jewish organizations in the United States have had our own challenges in overcoming what divides us and uniting over what is most important.

The Book of Psalms calls upon Jews to make Jerusalem their top priority, "elevating it above our foremost joy." That line is recited at the peak of traditional Jewish wedding ceremonies, emphasizing that Jerusalem should always be at the forefront of the concerns of the Jewish people – in times of distress and also in times of our greatest joy.

In an event organized by the Religious Zionists of America, the anniversary of Jerusalem's reunification will soon be marked in the halls of Congress.

The event will be co-sponsored and addressed by both the Democratic and Republican leadership, proving that like the Jewish state as a whole, Jerusalem unites our very divided representatives on Capitol Hill.

Besides uniting the bipartisan leadership on a political level, the event will also bring together representatives of the Jewish community from across many divides. It is co-sponsored by 25 disparate organizations that are not always on the same page.

By coming together to celebrate the unity of Jerusalem, these Jewish organizations are not only marking a miracle, they are also perpetuating one.

They are demonstrating appreciation to God for His miracles and to the great leadership of the United States for its tremendous support for Israel and its undivided capital.

The recent passage of United Nations Security Council Resolution 2334, which undermines Israel's control over Jerusalem's Old City and denies 3,000 years of history, underscores the importance of the event in Washington.

The event gives hope that just as now, when we will be coming together to celebrate Jerusalem's unity, if there will ever again be a time of concern for the future of Jerusalem, the leaders of Israel, its allies in Washington and American Jewish leaders and the communities they represent will stand together, united as one.

The Jerusalem Post

Push for embassy move to Jerusalem with head held high

The truth is that moving the embassy will make the world safer, because it will tell the world that America will honor its commitments to its allies.

MAY 21, 2017

In a parting interview with The Jerusalem Post six years ago, Arizona Senator Jon Kyl said his biggest regret in three decades of public service was adding a presidential waiver to the Jerusalem Embassy Act that he authored in 1995.

The law requires the US to move its embassy in Israel to Jerusalem and passed by a 93 to five vote, despite the objection of president Bill Clinton. But the waiver enables American presidents to suspend implementation of the law for six months. Kyl said he was a brandnew senator then, so he let himself be talked into it by veteran pro-Israel senators.

"What I regret is that when we did this, we were told that it couldn't happen by 'friends' of Israel in the Senate who insisted that they would be supportive as long as the waiver was included," Kyl recalled. "I should have tested them and seen if they would have voted against it without the waiver. In a spirit of reconciliation, I put in the waiver, and the rest is history."

President Barack Obama signed the last waiver in December. That means moving the embassy has been delayed to the end of May.

To honor his commitment that he made throughout his campaign to move America's embassy from Tel Aviv to the capital, President Donald Trump does not have to do anything at all. He just has to let June 1 arrive without signing another waiver.

"We will move the American embassy to the eternal capital of the Jewish people, Jerusalem," Trump said in his speech to the AIPAC Policy Conference in March 2016. "We will send a clear signal that there is no daylight between America and our most reliable ally, the State of Israel."

Trump's ambassador to Israel, David Friedman, went further, telling the crowd at a pro-Trump rally in Jerusalem's Old City on October 26 that if State Department workers refused to move the embassy, Trump would stand up to them using the catch-phrase from his reality television show: "You're fired!"

The president reportedly intended to announce that he was moving the embassy immediately after the inauguration, but was persuaded not to by Jordanian King Abdullah and other opponents of the move. Now is the time to persuade Trump not to sign the waiver and let the embassy move take place. If Trump signs the waiver once, he will sign it every six months, and it will become routine. And who knows who the next president will be? So the next several weeks before June 1 are crucial.

The Jerusalem Embassy Act gives 17 reasons why the embassy should be moved, including that every sovereign nation under international law and custom may designate its own capital and that Jerusalem is home to Israel's president, parliament and Supreme Court. The law also gives formal recognition by America that Jerusalem is Israel's capital.

The law noted that a year later, in 1996, the State of Israel would celebrate the 3,000th anniversary of the Jewish presence in Jerusalem since King David's entry. Now that another anniversary is being marked, 50 years since the city's reunification in 1967, it is the perfect time to implement the law.

Vice President Mike Pence told American Jewish leaders celebrating Israel's Independence Day in the Eisenhower Executive Office Building next to the White House that Trump was still giving "serious consideration" to moving the embassy.

Now is the time for American supporters of Israel to press the administration to make the right decision. The way we preserve Jerusalem is to urge the administration to move the embassy.

The Book of Psalms calls for making Jerusalem one's top priority, "elevating it above our foremost joy." That line is recited at the peak of traditional Jewish wedding ceremonies. Just as the psalm says we cannot forget Jerusalem, we also cannot be silent about our capital.

We must counter-balance those who have warned of an international conflagration if the simple act is undertaken of putting a sign on America's consulate in Jerusalem that says "embassy" and a sign on the embassy in Tel Aviv that says "consulate."

The truth is that moving the embassy will make the world safer, because it will tell the world that America will honor its commitments to its allies. Countries around the world will see the US reward Israel, its ultimate ally, and know that after eight years when it was unclear, they now must be on America's side.

In 1967, Menachem Begin said that if Israel did not take advantage of the historic opportunity to retake the Old City and reunite Jerusalem, future generations would not forgive them. That is also true at this moment. Just as Begin said then, "We have in our hands a gift of history," the same may hold true now with Trump.

"Jerusalem, the city that has become bound together, the eternal capital of Israel and of the Land of Israel, shall not be subjected to any division and is our liberated and indivisible capital and so it shall remain from generation to generation," he said.

The Jewish Press

Jerusalem: the capital of Israel

MAY 30, 2017

In a parting interview with The Jerusalem Post six years ago, Arizona Senator Jon Kyl said his biggest regret in three decades of public service was adding a presidential waiver to the Jerusalem Embassy Act that he authored in 1995.

The law requires the US to move its embassy in Israel to Jerusalem and passed by a 93 to five vote, despite the objection of president Bill Clinton. But the waiver enables American presidents to suspend implementing the law for six months. Kyl said he was a brand-new senator then, so he let himself be talked into it by veteran pro-Israel senators.

"What I regret is that when we did this, we were told that it couldn't happen by 'friends' of Israel in the Senate who insisted that they would be supportive as long as the waiver was included," Kyl recalled. "I should have tested them and seen if they would have voted against it without the waiver. In a spirit of reconciliation, I put in the waiver, and the rest is history."

President Barack Obama signed the last waiver in December. That means moving the embassy has been delayed to the end of May.

To honor his commitment that he made throughout his campaign to move America's embassy from Tel Aviv to the capital, President Donald Trump does not have to do anything at all. He just has to let June 1 arrive without signing another waiver.

"We will move the American embassy to the eternal capital of the Jewish people, Jerusalem," Trump said in his speech to the AIPAC Policy Conference in March 2016. "We will send a clear signal that there is no daylight between America and our most reliable ally, the State of Israel."

Trump's ambassador to Israel David Friedman went further, telling the crowd at a pro-Trump rally in Jerusalem's Old City on October 26 that if State Department workers refused to move the embassy, Trump would stand up to them using the catch-phrase from his reality television show: "You're fired!"

The president reportedly intended to announce that he was moving the embassy immediately after the inauguration, but he was persuaded not to by Jordanian King Abdullah and other opponents of the move.

Now is the time to persuade Trump not to sign the waiver and let the embassy move take place. If Trump signs the waiver once, he will sign it every six months, and it will become routine. And who knows who the next president will be? So the next several weeks before June 1 are crucial.

The Jerusalem Embassy Act gives 17 reasons why the capital should be moved, including that every sovereign nation under international law and custom may designate its own capital and that Jerusalem is home to Israel's president, parliament and Supreme Court. The law also gives formal recognition by America that Jerusalem is Israel's capital.

The law noted that a year later, in 1996, the State of Israel would celebrate the 3,000th anniversary of the Jewish presence in Jerusalem since King David's entry. Now that another anniversary is being marked, 50 years since the city's reunification in 1967, it is the perfect time to implement the law.

Vice President Mike Pence told American Jewish leaders celebrating Israel's Independence Day in the Eisenhower Executive Office Building next to the White House that Trump was still giving "serious consideration" to moving the embassy.

Now is the time for American supporters of Israel to press the administration to make the right decision. The way we preserve Jerusalem is to urge the administration to move the embassy.

The Book of Psalms calls for making Jerusalem one's top priority, "elevating it above our foremost joy." That line is recited at the peak of traditional Jewish wedding ceremonies. Just as the psalm says we cannot forget Jerusalem, we also cannot be silent about our capital.

We must counter-balance those who have warned of an international conflagration if the simple act is undertaken of putting a sign on America's consulate in Jerusalem that says embassy and a sign on the embassy in Tel Aviv that says consulate.

The truth is that moving the embassy will make the world safer, because it will tell the world that America will honor its commitments to its allies. Countries around the world will see the U.S. reward Israel, its ultimate ally, and know that after eight years when it was unclear, they now must be on America's side.

In 1967, Menachem Begin said that if Israel did not take advantage of the historic opportunity to retake the Old City and reunite Jerusalem, future generations would not forgive them. That is also true at this moment. Just as Begin said then "We have in our hands a gift of history," the same may hold true now with Trump.

"Jerusalem, the city that has become bound together, the eternal capital of Israel and of the Land of Israel, shall not be subjected to any division and is our liberated and indivisible capital and so it shall remain from generation to generation," he said.

The Jerusalem Post

Equivocating on Qatar

Qatar must also immediately stop its support of terrorist organizations and end its alliance with Iran, the world's worst sponsor of terrorism.

SEPTEMBER 24, 2017

The United Nations General Assembly has historically led to unexpected meetings. A series of meetings this week between American Jewish leaders and Qatari Emir Sheikh Tamim bin Hamad Al Thani and other members of his family on the sidelines of the GA has been no exception. The meetings have raised challenging ethical questions.

On the one hand, Qatar is one of the world's primary sponsors of terrorism. It funds Hamas, as well as branches of the Muslim Brotherhood in other Arab countries that threaten the State of Israel. Why would those who oppose Israel speaking to Hamas run to meet with its primary sponsor? On the other hand, Qatar, like Israel, is a small state threatened by its neighboring enemies, Saudi Arabia and the United Arab Emirates in the case of Qatar, who reportedly would have attacked were it not for a warning from US President Donald Trump.

It hosts a large US air base, and once featured an Israeli trade office. Trump himself has warned that the dispute between Qatar and its neighbors must not be allowed to distract US allies from forging a united front against Iran.

Maybe by engaging the Qataris, Jewish leaders can help lead the world's richest country from the dark side to the light. Indeed, we speak to Turkey, which has been no less a sponsor of terrorism under President Recep Tayyip Erdogan, and praise Saudi crown prince Mohammad bin Salman, whose country treats women much worse than Qatar does.

Besides, what harm can be caused by simply talking? That question can be answered by observing the success of Qatar's international television network Al-Jazeera.

Al-Jazeera covers the Middle East more than any other media outlet. Reaching out to the Arab world in Arabic and the rest of the world in English, it spreads Qatar's agenda to the entire international community.

That agenda includes empowering the Muslim Brotherhood, replacing the Palestinian Authority with Hamas, and destroying the State of Israel. Practically, none of those goals can be accomplished without an army, but years of skewed media coverage can certainly make a major impact.

That coverage may soon be tested, because Palestinian Authority chairman Mahmoud Abbas is 82, continues to chain-smoke, and is not in good health. It is imperative to US Jews that Qatar not succeed in its goal of having Hamas take over the PA.
Each US Jewish leader can, of course, make his or her own decision about whether to engage or boycott the Qataris. But those who choose to interact must insist on Qatar immediately changing course.

One way to start is for Qatar to mediate the release of the bodies of IDF soldiers Hadar Goldin and Oron Shaul, which Hamas has held since Operation Protective Edge in October 2014. Such a move would demonstrate to the world that Qatar can be a force for good if Doha is brought into the camp.

Qatar must also immediately stop its support of terrorist organizations and end its alliance with Iran, the world's worst sponsor of terrorism. Reopening Israel's trade office would be another key step.

We Jews believe in the concept of repentance, especially at this time of Rosh Hashana and Yom Kippur. That concept applies not only to individuals but also to countries, whom we believe are also judged by God at this time of year.

The answer to the moral question of meeting with Qatar is the same as the answer to many of the questions in the Middle East: it's complicated.

The Jerusalem Post

Skeptical of Saudi Arabia

Close ties between bin-Salman and his unofficial counterpart in the US, Jared Kushner, were seen as the basis for US President Donald Trump making Saudi Arabia and Israel the two first countries he visited as president five months ago.

OCTOBER 23, 2017

Because of his relative open-mindedness, Saudi Crown Prince Mohammed bin Salman has become the darling of the pro-Israel community. As he takes steps to wean Saudi Arabia off oil, he is believed to view Israel's economy as a model for that of his own country. For years, there have been reports of his contacts with Israeli officials. There is even speculation that he made a discreet visit to the Jewish state in early September.

Close ties between bin-Salman and his unofficial counterpart in the US, Jared Kushner, were seen as the basis for US President Donald Trump making Saudi Arabia and Israel the two first countries he visited as president five months ago.

Notwithstanding the above, Israel and American Jews must proceed cautiously with their coronation of the Saudis as reliable allies. History has proven that in the Middle East, the enemy of your enemy – in this case Iran – is not necessarily your friend.

The Economist reported last month that bin-Salman has been reaching out to Iranian allies and speculated that genuine Sunni- Shi'ite rapprochement was on the way. The report spoke of a "grand bargain" between Saudi Arabia and Iran, in which the Saudis would accept Iranian domination of Syria in return for a free hand in the Gulf states.

"We are ready to cooperate with Saudi Arabia to put an end to violence in Syria, to violence and oppression in Bahrain, not to mention the irrational war in Yemen," Iranian Foreign Minister Mohammad Javad

Zarif told the pan-Arabist satellite TV channel Al-Mayadeen in an interview last month.

There were 85,000 Iranian pilgrims who participated in this year's pilgrimage to Mecca. Iraqi Interior Minister Qasim al-Araji told reporters in Tehran on August 13 that Saudi officials had asked his government to help their country mend ties with Iran.

It should be noted that the fickle crown prince, who has reversed key Saudi policies before, could do the same regarding Iran, especially under pressure from the Russians, with whom the Saudi leadership has become increasingly close in recent months despite a long history of distrust between the two countries. Indeed, the Russians like playing the "Iran card" against the US and could use Saudi assistance in doing so.

No one knows what happened behind the scenes in last month's first-ever meeting in Russia of a Saudi king and a Russian president. Perhaps during the four-day visit King Salman and Russian President Vladimir Putin were working on that rapprochement between Saudi Arabia and Iran, or at least on enabling Iran to receive the foothold in Syria that Israel has begged Putin to refrain from giving the Islamic Republic.

Given Putin's reputation for stubbornness, it is more likely that the Saudis deferred to Russian demands on Iran rather than vice versa. During the meetings in Russia, Saudi Arabia reportedly acknowledged that Russian domination of Syria and its growing regional influence would continue. The Saudis reportedly also made huge purchases of arms in Moscow, providing a much needed boost to the stagnating Russian economy.

Putin has been trying to improve his ties with the Saudis since he took power in 2000. He became the first Russian leader to visit Riyadh in 2007, at a time when the Saudis were upset with the US due to its war in Iraq and America's support for a Shi'ite government in Baghdad. Saudi relations with the US had been cooling since 2003, when the Saudis forced the relocation of US personnel from the Prince Sultan Air Base, which once hosted 60,000 Americans.

On a spring visit to Moscow, bin-Salman said relations between his country and Russia were better than ever. When he first met with Putin in 2015, it resulted in the Saudi "sovereign wealth fund" committing to invest an unprecedented $10 billion in Russia over five years. Seen as an attempt by the Saudis to bribe the Russians, Putin ultimately rejected the offer.

The 32-year-old crown prince's lavish lifestyle and provocative personality have faced criticism. His lecturing of then-US president Barack Obama about the failures of American foreign policy two years ago has not been forgotten, and his war in Yemen has not been successful. Thousands of lives and tens of billions of dollars have been lost in that war, which has failed to defeat the Shi'ite Houthis.

Congress has been trying to end the Saudi participation in the Arab boycott of Israel unsuccessfully for years. Women may finally be allowed to drive in Saudi Arabia next June, but their cars won't have Mobileye collision prevention technology, because it comes from Israel.

All of this should signal a warning light to Israel and its supporters in the United States: in reaching a relationship with Israel, the Saudis still have a long way to go and in fact may never get there.

The Jerusalem Post

The force to end terrorism

There are many ways to fight terrorism. But there are also steps that can be taken by our lawmakers.

NOVEMBER 23, 2017

Twenty-nine-year-old US Army veteran Cpt. Taylor Allen Force had served his country in Iran and Afghanistan, but did not die in battle. The Lubbock, Texas native and West Point graduate was murdered walking on a beach promenade while on a Vanderbilt University graduate school trip abroad in March 2016.

The site of his murder was Jaffa, Israel, but it could have happened in London, Paris, or Texas. In the past, jihadist terrorism primarily targeted Jews in Israel, but now it hits anywhere and anyone, terrorizing innocent civilians around the world.

There is no better symbol for the war on terrorism than Taylor Force. He fought bravely for America in his life, fell victim to terrorism in his death and now lives on as the inspiration for efforts to defeat terrorism.

There are many ways to fight terrorism. Most involve proactive and reactive offensive and defensive steps by militaries, law enforcement authorities and intelligence agencies. But there are also steps that can be taken by our lawmakers.

The Taylor Force Act, sponsored by Republican senators Lindsey Graham and Bob Corker and co-sponsored by top Democrats, would require the Palestinian Authority to stop compensating convicted terrorists and their families or face a freeze in aid from the United States.

The bill would demand that the PA end its "pay for slay" policy that resulted in Force's murderer's family receiving a hefty monthly stipend, like other families of terrorists.

The PA distributed some $300 million to the families of terrorists in 2016, coincidentally the same sum the US annually provides the PA.

"Taylor was an American hero who was brutally murdered at the hands of terrorists," Graham said. "Yet instead of condemning this horrific attack – and so many others like it – the PA rewards terrorists. These rewards for terrorist attacks are inconsistent with American values. They are inconsistent with decency. And they are certainly inconsistent with peace. Simply put, you can't be a partner in peace when you are paying people to commit acts of terror. It is long past time to let the PA know that these practices are wholly unacceptable."

Much like sanctions on Iran that harmed its economy and removing Iran from the international banking system caused the Islamic Republic to make concessions, a financial game plan can be successful with the Palestinians. Terrorist organizations cannot succeed without financial support, so they must be isolated financially.

The bill has been advancing in the Senate and the House of Representatives, thanks to its broad, bipartisan support and the backing and moral clarity of US President Donald Trump. Support from both sides of the aisle cannot be taken for granted nowadays and proves that there is a consensus in America on there being zero tolerance for terrorism.

A similar bill has been proposed in the Knesset. There, too, it enjoys the support of the entire political spectrum, which in the Jewish state is also no easy feat.

But the bills in both countries have faced roadblocks. In the US, some Democratic leaders have insisted on watering down the bill and granting the PA too long a time to stop funding terrorism. There is an effort to add to the bill a sunset clause that could allow the PA to return to funding terrorists.

It is possible that if and when an American Middle East peace plan is announced, the bill will be shelved. This would be a tragic mistake, because terrorism must be fought without regard to diplomatic efforts.

In Israel, the bill has run into games of bureaucracy and political credit.

It was proposed by MK Elazar Stern of the Yesh Atid party. Stern, who supports sweeping legislation on matters of religion and state, is anathema to most Orthodox MKs. For the bill to move forward, it needs the support of the Defense Ministry, led by defense minister and Yisrael Beytenu party head Avigdor Liberman.

Knesset Foreign Affairs and Defense Committee head Avi Dichter (Likud) complained that the Defense Ministry is stalling the bill, while meanwhile Israel continues to give the PA NIS 1.2 billion in tax and tariff revenues Israel collects for the PA every year.

A terrorism victims' organization has started a campaign against Liberman. Dichter pointed a finger at the Defense Ministry representative who testified to his committee.

"Five months have passed, and the cabinet ministries still haven't presented my committee with legislation that would freeze the funds the PA pays to terrorists," Dichter said. "We see a fire approaching, we have a supertanker that could put it out, and you are telling us to wait."

Dichter's statement should apply both in Israel and the US. It should be common sense that terrorism cannot be tolerated. How can the US keep on giving so much money to terrorists when it is fighting terrorism?

After the US helped defeat Islamic State, the war on terrorism continues. In the spirit of Taylor Force, now is the time for the US to win.

The Jerusalem Post

Recognizing all of Jerusalem, here to stay

Consequently, there is no bigger blow to terrorism against Israel, the US and the world than Trump's announcement.

DECEMBER 7, 2017

When President Donald Trump arrived in Israel in May, he was greeted by my article in The Jerusalem Post that called upon him to start the process of moving the US Embassy to Israel's capital.

I also called on American Jews to do their part in bringing about such a historic step.

"Now is the time for American supporters of Israel to press the administration to make the right decision," I wrote in the article that day.

"The way we preserve Jerusalem is to urge the administration to move the embassy."

It took six months longer than it should have, but President Trump should be commended for the move he announced on Wednesday, and American Jews should be patted on the back for their role in making it happen.

Trump's decisions demonstrate stronger than ever the massive power of the American Jewish community when it is able to set aside its differences and unite for an important cause.

Contrary to how Trump's announcement has been portrayed in the international media, I believe it will advance the cause of peace and the international effort against terrorism.

There is no step that demonstrates better to the world that the US will reward its allies and punish its enemies than America moving the embassy of Israel, its ultimate ally, to Jerusalem, its united, eternal capital.

Consequently, there is no bigger blow to terrorism against Israel, the US and the world than Trump's announcement.

Regardless of their opinion of Trump's policies on domestic issues, antisemitism and other elements in his foreign policy, US Jewish leaders must credit Trump for restoring American exceptionalism on Israel.

But the work is not done. We can still not afford to rest on our laurels.

Now that Jerusalem has been recognized by the US president as Israel's capital, questions remain regarding what Jerusalem will be.

Will Israel be forced to relinquish sizable portions of its capital as part of a diplomatic process with an enemy that has not given up its hope of destroying the Jewish state? Will the development of Israel's largest city continue to be stifled artificially by the international community falsely defining its largest northern and southern neighborhoods and its suburbs on three sides as Jewish settlements? Should Jerusalem continue to remain one of the few capitals in the world that does not have an airport? Even well-meaning MKs on the Right, such as the Likud's Anat Berko, have recently proposed relinquishing neighborhoods in Jerusalem just because they are overwhelmingly Arab. Berko's plan calls for unilaterally relinquishing control over 22 square kilometers in Jerusalem where 300,000 Arabs and very few Jews live.

This is not the time for making concessions in Israel's capital. It is the time to grow and solidify the city for its residents of all religions and ethnicities, and sectors, and to call for people around the world to come and pray.

We Jews have yearned for Jerusalem for more than 1,800 years, and now it is miraculously back under our control.

True salvation for Jerusalem will not come from DC but from us realizing that it is DC – David's City, and it is therefore our obligation to preserve, maintain, and cherish all of it.

The Jerusalem Post

Appreciating Israel's miracle at 70 with unity

The light that the Nazis tried unsuccessfully to extinguish is now brighter than ever.

JANUARY 8, 2018

Pirkei Avot teaches that a 70-year-old has reached a "ripe old age" ("seiva" in Hebrew), a term used in the Book of Chronicles to describe King David, who died at age 70.

On Yom Ha'atzmaut, Israel's Independence Day (April 19), the Jewish State will become 70, with hopes for a long future ahead.

During those seven decades, Israel's population has grown from 806,000 to 8.68 million, and its main export has shifted from oranges to hi-tech start-ups purchased by Apple.

A country started by destitute people with no experience in farming made the desert bloom, beleaguered Holocaust survivors built the IDF into a strong army, and there are now more people studying Torah in the land of Israel than ever before, despite the loss of Europe's Torah teachers.

The light that the Nazis tried unsuccessfully to extinguish is now brighter than ever. Israel is striving to be the light unto the nations that its prophets predicted.

On Hanukka, Jews are commanded to light their hanukkiot in the window where their neighbors can see them, in order to "publicize the miracle." On Yom Ha'atzmaut, we should behave similarly.

We should want the world to see Jews around the world celebrating the miracle of Israel turning 70 against all odds and thriving despite all logic. The best way to publicize the miracle is to bring Jews together to unite behind Israel.

History has proven that when Israel faces challenges of war, Jews around the world have been able to set aside their differences and come together to help ensure the country's survival. But families must also come together in good times and celebrate what God gave them.

Religious Zionists in particular believe in thanking God for the modern State of Israel. We endured 1,878 years of exile with no state to save the Jewish people from pogroms, crusades, inquisitions and the Holocaust.

We can see the contrast of what happens when we have a state of our own to absorb Jewish immigrants from the four corners of the earth. Israel took in a million people from the Former Soviet Union, brought Africans to the promised land on the wings of eagles, and became a destination for aliya by choice of Americans seeking better quality of life.

When Prime Minister Benjamin Netanyahu addressed the United Nations General Assembly, he said he had visited six continents in a year and a half, because the world wants to know about Israel's expertise in innovation and its unfortunate experience in successfully fighting terrorism.

The world has also been seeking out Israel due to its natural gas discoveries off its coast after decades of believing incorrectly that the Land of Israel was not blessed with the most lucrative natural resources.

The world leaders Netanyahu meets with often still criticize Israel, but that has become a small part of a larger conversation, as the world realizes more and more how much Israel has to offer.

The fact that, amid all that success, there are too many poor Israelis being left behind means that there is still much to be done by the Jewish Diaspora to support Israel, even as the relationship becomes more of a two-way street.

Politics must not be permitted to get in the way of that relationship. Just like we do not always understand all the decisions made by our children, we must continue showing them love.

Israel remains a work in progress, as its politicians and world renowned legal system continue their give and take, figuring out what it means to be a Jewish, Democratic state. "Israel" itself means struggling with God, in both present and future tense.

The messiah has not yet come and brought about the prophecy of 70 nations from around the world coming to Zion (though former president Shimon Peres's funeral came close). That miracle has not yet transpired.

So the Religious Zionist of America have decided to bring 70 inspiring speakers from Israel to speak on the Shabbat before Yom Ha'atzmaut in North America's 70 largest Orthodox synagogues. Those communities will be marking the milestone of Israel's 70th birthday by expressing gratitude to God in their prayers and learning from their Israeli guests about the Jewish state's bright future.

The Jerusalem Post

Bringing Qatar into the fold

"I wanted to persuade the Qataris that they could play a more positive role on the Palestinian issue and stop helping Hamas."

FEBRUARY 21, 2018

There are not too many Orthodox Jews who have been to both the United Arab Emirates and Qatar, let alone been welcomed as a guest of the government in both Persian Gulf States.

I received criticism for visiting Qatar, as have other American Jewish leaders who have gone there recently, even though most of them have either withheld judgment or criticized Qatar upon their return.

I accepted the invitation, because I wanted to persuade the Qataris that they could play a more positive role on the Palestinian issue and stop helping Hamas.

I wanted to hear their side of the story. Perhaps their negative image was unjustified. I was dubious about Qatar being different from any of the other Arab states. Intuitively, I thought none of them could be trusted and that Qatar could be no worse than Saudi Arabia.

My visit to the UAE came last week, along with other Jewish leaders from the Conference of Presidents of Major American Jewish Organizations, though I arrived a few days earlier to explore the emirates.

Visiting both countries in a short period gave me perspective that I believe could have an influence on Qatar, which is striving to improve its image in the world, especially among American decision-makers.

Qatar and the UAE have many similarities and many key differences.

They are both small former British colonies that in a short period built themselves up into technologically super-advanced, massively wealthy, family-run sheikhdoms, thanks to their vast natural resources. Both have increasingly influential economies diversifying away from oil. In both, native citizens are less than 10% of the total population.

And both are currently investing heavily in re-branding themselves for the US in general and the Trump administration in particular, in high-stakes campaigns that have attracted attention and controversy.

The UAE has succeeded in that goal, developing close relations with American governments from both parties, deepening military ties, expanding trade with the US to $26 billion, and building its most populous city, Dubai, into a financial metropolis with a skyline that reminded me of Manhattan. The UAE is also a close ally of Saudi Arabia, and together they are waging an active war with Iran's Houthi proxy in Yemen.

Sheikh Mohamed bin Zayed Al-Nahyan, called MbZ, is UAE's crown prince and deputy supreme commander of its armed forces. He is seen as the driving force behind the UAE's activist foreign policy, promoting diversity and tolerance, shunning radicalization and deepening close ties with his Saudi and American counterparts, Saudi Crown Prince Mohammad bin Salman and Jared Kushner.

In dialogue with our interlocutors in Abu Dhabi, it became clear that – with rare exceptions – the UAE is doing its part to be a positive force in the Middle East. But the UAE needs its Saudi allies to do their part as a regional force and lead efforts against Iran and its terrorist proxies.

Qatar's progress in winning over America has been slower. US President Donald Trump called Qatari Emir Sheikh Tamim bin Hamad al-Thani last month to thank him for helping fight terrorism. By hosting an American air base (built after the US was asked to leave Saudi Arabia) with fighter jets used for air strikes on Islamic State, Qatar can rightfully say it hosts the US fight on terrorism.

But unfortunately, Qatar also remains a safe haven for some of the world's terrorist groups, harboring Hamas, the Muslim Brotherhood and others. It is not doing enough to pressure Hamas to release Israeli captives, dead and alive.

The Al-Jazeera network is based in the Qatari capital Doha, and its biased and problematic coverage does not advance the cause of Middle East peace, to put it mildly. For those reasons and more there has been such an outcry over the visits to Qatar.

Qatar justifies its behavior by noting that its sovereignty and even its existence is threatened by the Iranians, Saudis and the Emirates. It explains that it must get along with Iran, because it shares lucrative gas fields with the Islamic Republic.

But the Qataris must realize that their long-term strategic interests require shunning Iran, fighting the terrorism emanating from the Islamic Republic and seeking a full alliance with the US. After all, Iran's primary goal is to defeat all Sunni states and control the world, and when it tries to exercise that plan, due to its proximity, Qatar will be among its first targets.

They can look to the UAE and see the benefits their neighbor has received from fighting alongside the US and never against it in all operations throughout the Middle East. The UAE was even willing to make sacrifices for their alliance, starting the process of stopping trade with Iran and losing business deals there to Turkey.

Among the steps that could help Qatar win over America would be to adopt a policy of not tolerating any terrorism, work behind the scenes with the US against Iran, pressure the Palestinians to return to the negotiating table under American mediation, and provide humanitarian assistance to Gaza through Israel and aid organizations to ensure it really reaches the people and is not stolen by Hamas.

As all American allies in the region should, Qatar could fund educational initiatives that encourage tolerance, end incitement to terrorism, promote human rights, and even use Al-Jazeera to promote the positive messages that the Middle East needs today.

None of America's current and potential allies are perfect. They could all do more.

The Trump administration should also do its part to unify the Gulf states against terrorism, because for the war on terrorism to succeed there cannot be any outliers. There must be complete unity.

The Jerusalem Post

In praise of Trump's Passover cleaning

The Passover Haggada states that in every generation, the Jewish people has had enemies who have attempted to destroy it, but God intervened and saved it.

MARCH 29, 2018

There were jokes on social media about how having an Orthodox Jewish daughter and son-in-law had influenced US President Donald Trump to clean out his cabinet before Passover.

But the recent departure of Secretary of State Rex Tillerson and National Security Adviser H.R. McMaster is good news for the world's two most important international initiatives that go hand in hand: Stopping the nuclearization of Iran and the terrorism emanating from the Islamic Republic.

Tillerson regularly deemed Iran as complying with the 2015 landmark Iran nuclear deal, though not with its "spirit." He had urged Trump to maintain the agreement, in order to preserve American leverage over the development of Iranian ballistic missiles and other key issues.

McMaster was known for advising the president not to shun multilateral cooperation. He was also in favor of finding ways to keep the Iran deal.

Trump singled out Tillerson's inability to see eye to eye with him on Iran as the primary reason for his firing. From now on, only the Iran policies Trump believes in will be advanced by his administration.

That means the deal will have to either be "fixed or nixed," as Prime Minister Benjamin Netanyahu told the United Nations General Assembly in September. Energy Minister Yuval Steinitz, who is close to Netanyahu, told The Jerusalem Post that if the deal is properly fixed, it could even be extended to ensure its sunset clauses remain far in the distance.

The Tillerson and McMaster firings sent a key message to Europe that America is serious about the need for dramatic steps. Immediately after Trump fired McMaster on Twitter, the three European signatories to the deal – Britain, France and Germany – agreed to new EU sanctions on Iran's ballistic missile program and to punish Iran for its involvement in the Syrian civil war.

Netanyahu told German and French foreign ministers that he thinks Trump will pull out of the deal. But there is new hope that an agreement on sanctions and increased inspections of Iranian nuclear sites that can be acceptable to Israel can be reached by the May 12 deadline set by the Trump administration.

The Trump administration is finally succeeding in fixing the greatest mistake of President Barack Obama that could still lead to Iran being able to cast a nuclear shadow over the Middle East and the entire world.

In his quest to reach what became the Joint Comprehensive Plan of Action, Obama turned a blind eye to Iranian aggression in Yemen, Iraq, Lebanon and Syria.

He did not make it a priority to stop the spread of Iranian-backed terrorism perpetrated by Hezbollah in Lebanon, Hamas in the Gaza Strip and throughout the world.

Now, the clear message from the White House is there is no longer any tolerance for terrorism and that the entire international community must get its act together, because the war on terror is moving forward full speed ahead.

That means targeting Iran, the world's primary sponsor of terrorism, whose surrogates cause chaos throughout the Middle East.

Incoming secretary of state Mike Pompeo recognizes the dangers of radical Islamic terrorism and is unafraid to speak those words, unlike Obama and the secretaries of state who worked under him.

Incoming US national security adviser John Bolton has urged for both American and Israeli military action against Iran.

To that end, they will work closely with Netanyahu, whom Tillerson did not visit when he came to the Middle East, and with Saudi Crown Prince Muhammad bin Salman, who just had a successful trip to Washington.

The prince is the key to stopping terrorism emanating from Iran and preventing its nuclearization.

He has accused Supreme Leader Ayatollah Ali Khamenei of being the "new Hitler" of the Middle East, because Khamenei wants to expand Iranian rule over neighboring countries. But Muhammad's own desire for a nuclear capability and his warnings that if Iran develops a nuclear weapon, Saudi Arabia will follow suit shortly thereafter, have been very unhelpful.

How can a volatile Middle East be unified against Iran when Saudi Arabia's own motives will be questioned? This is especially problematic when Saudi leadership in the efforts against Iran is so crucial.

It will now be up to Pompeo and Bolton to keep Prince Muhammad in line and influence President Trump to make the right decisions on Iran.

The Passover Haggada states that in every generation, the Jewish people has had enemies who have attempted to destroy it, but God intervened and saved it.

Perhaps in retrospect, this changing of the guard in the Trump cabinet will be remembered as a key instrument in God's saving Israel from nuclear annihilation and the world from the spread of terrorism.

The Jerusalem Post

Looking ahead to Jerusalem's future

No city around the world can truly copy Jerusalem.

APRIL 8, 2018

Jerusalem Mayor Nir Barkat announced his decision to enter national politics and not seek a third term as mayor last month.

Barkat's departure set off immediate speculation regarding who could replace him and run Israel's complex capital. It is far too early to say whether Barkat's successor will come from among the current candidates or whether someone not yet the subject of speculation will sweep the holy city off its feet.

But with all due respect to politics, there has been far less speculation about what vision will be adopted for the future of the city.

Barkat's vision was clear and transparent. He was a hi-tech-focused venture capitalist. In May 2015, he unveiled Jerusalem 2020, a five-year plan written by Harvard professor Michael Porter.

The plan focuses on creating more jobs, culture, and public transportation. Its main recommendations were to build a hi-tech park around Hebrew University's Givat Ram campus and an international center for in-vitro fertilization at Jerusalem's hospitals.

While the initiators of such ideas clearly meant well, this cookie-cutter kind of plan could be implemented on any continent, and it was not built for the special character of the birthplace of the world's three leading religions. Jerusalem's development will not come from another office building that could fit well in Cincinnati, Sydney, or Stockholm.

Jerusalem Affairs Minister Ze'ev Elkin also has a plan. It calls for abandoning all Arab neighborhoods located over the security barrier and creating a new municipal council to govern them. Residents of such neighborhoods would no longer be able to vote in municipal elections, which would preserve the Jewish majority of Israel's capital.

That plan, too, has flaws. Politics aside, shrinking the city makes less sense than building it into a larger metropolis by taking over the administration of adjacent successful communities.

Perhaps the most far-thinking vision presented in recent years is the Jerusalem 5800 plan, a private initiative of Australian Jewish philanthropist and businessman Kevin Bermeister. It focuses on what the city could look like in 2050, corresponding to 5800 in the Jewish calendar.

This intriguing and ambitious plan calls for focusing on the 3,000 years of history in the holy city to draw in 10 million tourists annually from around the world and two million from inside Israel. That would be a massive rise over the current 1.5 million.

To that end, Jerusalem would need to at least quadruple its current 10,000 hotel rooms by building new hotels throughout the city and the wider metropolis that extends to the Dead Sea. Tourism in the city would focus on its biblical heritage, preserving archaeological sites, developing historic Emek Refaim as a biblical-themed park, and recreating Jerusalem's biblical areas.

The plan also calls for building a major airport just outside the city. Jerusalem is one of the few capital cities in the world that lacks an airport, and it will need a large one to handle the massive influx of tourists, who with all due respect did not read about Tel Aviv or Lod in the Bible.

Tel Aviv recently unveiled a historic trail that takes visitors back to the city's beginnings ahead of the founding of the state. Jerusalem has a head start of nearly 4,000 years on Tel Aviv, going back to the binding of Isaac on the future site of the Holy Temples.

There are more than 67 million Christians in China, who can be attracted to walk in the path of Abraham. Special emphasis should be put on accommodating tourists from the Far East, which would require training those involved in the tourist industry in Jerusalem and drafting guides and other professionals who speak Chinese, Japanese and Korean. In 2016, a Chinese airline began direct service to Israel for the first time, and Air India's new ability to travel over Saudi Arabia is a revolutionary development.

A recent report revealed plans to build a Disneyland park in the southern development town of Dimona. Jerusalem does not need Mickey and Donald, because it has David and Solomon.

What is even more special about that is that no city around the world can truly copy Jerusalem. You cannot replicate where Jesus walked or Joseph had his dreams, and the 2,000-year-old exhibits throughout the city live on longer than any museum.

And while politics has held the city back for decades, the move of America's embassy to Israel's capital could signal a new wave of international recognition of Jerusalem that could give it a huge boost.

Let's hope that whoever wins the mayor's race realizes the potential of the city and implements the kind of winning, long-term vision that will allow its future residents to look back fondly not only on days of old but also on decisions made in our times.

The Jerusalem Post

Showing appreciation for blessings from Trump

In a world where promises are thrown out with no intention of ever being kept, seeing promises implemented nowadays is a breath of fresh air.

MAY 9, 2018

This weekend's Torah portion deals with the blessings and curses of the Jewish people.

Reading through the blessings and curses, it is remarkable to see how each and every one of the curses have unfortunately come true. Thankfully, nearly all the blessings have as well.

A notable exception is that we are still waiting for God's promise of peace in the Land of Israel. We will never give up our hope that God will keep His promise and that peace will be achieved.

As Jews, we are commanded to emulate God. That means that just as God keeps His promises, so must we. In fact, we must be so careful that when we make promises, we traditionally add the words "God willing" in English or the Hebrew words "bli neder," which literally means "without taking a vow."

In a world where promises are thrown out with no intention of ever being kept, seeing promises implemented nowadays is a breath of fresh air. Witnessing them maintained by a politician is even cause for celebration.

Throughout the American presidential election campaign, US President Donald Trump issued promise after promise to Jewish leaders.

He said he would end the international delegitimization of Israel, abandon the terrible Iran deal and move our embassy from Tel Aviv to Jerusalem.

He kept the first promise by sending Nikki Haley to the United Nations to fight against the institution being used for disproportionate Israel-bashing while ignoring the obvious abuses of some of the neighbors of the Jewish state. His administration stopped accusing Israel of occupying its own land.

The second promise was kept Tuesday, when Trump officially nixed the Iran deal.

In doing so, he cited the evidence provided by Israeli intelligence agencies, which was elucidated to the world by Prime Minister Benjamin Netanyahu. In his speech, President Trump said he wanted to send Iran a critical message that the United States no longer makes empty promises.

President Trump will keep his third promise Monday, when our embassy moves from Tel Aviv to Israel's capital, Jerusalem. In doing so, he will set himself apart from the many American presidents who made the same exact promise to Israel and American Jews and failed to keep it.

Perhaps it is no coincidence that the embassy is near the path that Abraham took to Jerusalem when he was on his way to sacrifice Isaac.

Abraham demonstrated the kind of commitment and faith that President Trump has been showing since he took office.

Rewarding Abraham for that commitment, God blessed him that his seed would be multiplied like the stars and the sand and that his descendants would inherit the cities of their enemies – similar blessings to what the Jews would later be promised, as recounted in this week's Torah portion.

President Trump also deserves to be blessed for his commitment. That commitment was reinforced by American Ambassador to Israel David Friedman, a proud religious Zionist and vocal Israel supporter, whose positive influence on the president must not be taken for granted. He must be commended for his successful efforts.

Deputy Minister Michael Oren said following the Iran speech that the president's announcement represented a chance for renewed Jewish unity after past rifts on the issue. The Jerusalem embassy move is an even greater unifying force for the people of Israel and Diaspora Jewry.

Regardless of one's feelings about the president's past behavior and domestic policies, one can hope that even the most liberal American Jews could show him the appreciation he deserves for demonstrating his commitment to Israel and the Jewish people so decisively.

That appreciation is called in Hebrew hakarat hatov, meaning "recognizing the good." We must recognize the good we received as a result of President Trump keeping his promises.

If we show enough of that appreciation, perhaps Israel will be even more worthy of the blessings predicted in the Torah portion that have already come true, and also the ultimate true peace.

The Jerusalem Post

A religious Zionist's praise for Isaac Herzog

Herzog learned from his grandfather how to be a mensch, and that is what the leadership of world Jewry requires more than ever.

JUNE 26, 2018

Shortly after the founding of the state, Israel's first Ashkenazi chief rabbi, Isaac Halevi Herzog, authored the Prayer for the Welfare of the State of Israel.

In the prayer, Herzog wrote that Israel would be "reshit tzmihat geulateinu ," the beginning of the blossoming of our redemption. Herzog's powerful words expressed the essence of Religious Zionism and are now the emotional highlight in synagogue services throughout the world, especially in challenging times for the State of Israel.

Seventy years later, Herzog's grandson and namesake, opposition leader Isaac Herzog, was selected as the new head of the Jewish Agency. His appointment surprised many, as did the support he received from Religious Zionists.

Prime Minister Benjamin Netanyahu opposed the appointment, and the only vote against Herzog in the selection committee that chose him came from the representative of World Likud.

But Bayit Yehudi leader Naftali Bennett praised the choice of Herzog, saying that "the Knesset lost a terrific parliamentarian, but the Jewish people gained a man of vision." Bennett said he trusted Herzog could build a new bridge between Israel and the Jews of the world.

World Zionist Organization chairman Avraham Duvdevani of the Religious Zionist Mizrachi told the agency's board of governors that "there can be no better candidate."
And I was quoted by this newspaper in February saying that "Herzog would make a great chairman of the Jewish Agency, because of his respect for Religious Zionism and understanding of Diaspora Jews."

That respect was one of many reasons Religious Zionists supported Herzog. His solid background was another.

Herzog went to the Religious Zionist Ramaz high school in New York, which prides itself on teaching its students to commit themselves to a life of Torah, mitzvot and support for the State of Israel.

Religious Zionists can be proud that a product of one of our schools rose through the ranks to become the head of the agency. He still regularly goes to a Religious Zionist synagogue in Tel Aviv.

Herzog is known for his ability to accomplish his goals quietly, behind the scenes. He is a man of compromise, at a time when all sides will have to let their guard down and put the good of the Jewish people first.

But most of all, he is a unifier. There are so many rifts that divide the Jewish people, the State of Israel, and how the two work together. He can help ease those rifts.

Herzog's ability to help his Jewish brothers get along comes from his Religious Zionist upbringing. Religious Zionists in Israel are proud to serve as the bridge between the secular and the haredim, understanding and respecting the needs of both.

He cares deeply about the future of Israel and the Jewish people, following in the footsteps of this father, Chaim Herzog, who as Israel's ambassador to the United Nations ripped up the UN resolution that Zionism is racism, and of his grandfather, who unsuccessfully met with then-US president Franklin Delano Roosevelt, in an effort to save the remnants of European Jewry.

Herzog learned from his grandfather how to be a mensch, and that is what the leadership of world Jewry requires more than ever.

So good luck, chairman Herzog. We will be praying for your success.

The Jerusalem Post

Response to a loving brother

Does Lauder believe that the administration of the late Yitzhak Rabin, which amended Basic Law: Human Dignity and Freedom without adding the magic word also tarnished Israel's equality?

AUGUST 19, 2018

World Jewish Congress president Ronald Lauder continued his unfortunate recent trend of criticizing the State of Israel's policies in The New York Times this week.

When he warned in a March op-ed in the Times that settlements endangered the two-state solution – and in his view, Israel's future – he wrote that he was speaking out as "a friend expressing an inconvenient truth."

This time, he wrote in the same newspaper "as a loving brother."

A true friend or brother would speak directly, as Lauder can, due to his closeness to Prime Minister Benjamin Netanyahu and other Israeli leaders, and then leave it up to them to make their choices about Israel's future, as their voters elected them to do.

Unfortunately, that is not what Lauder chose to do. Why is it friendly or brotherly to malign Israel on the pages of a newspaper with a long track record of criticizing Israel not only in its editorials but also in news fit and unfit to print?

This was out of character for Lauder, who has defended Israel in countries around the world for decades as the leader of the World Jewish Congress, Jewish National Fund and the Conference of Presidents of Major American Jewish Organizations. There is no gainsaying that Israel owes him a debt of gratitude for all he has done for the Jewish state.

One reason Lauder wrote for his criticism is the much-maligned Jewish Nation-State Law. But in the same newspaper, former Jerusalem Post editor-in-chief Bret Stephens pointed out that the bill's "most controversial provisions were stripped from it before passage" and that it is not "remotely as noxious as what is happening in other Western democracies wrestling with competing claims between national identity, civil liberties and cultural pluralism." He brought to attention worse legislation in Denmark and said the international community should reserve its outrage for Syria torturing hundreds of people to death.

Falling into the trap of opposition politicians in Israel and international media with an anti-Israel agenda, Lauder accuses the Knesset majority that passed the bill of "tarnishing equality," because that keyword is not in the new law. It is also not in any of the other Basic Laws passed by Israel, including Basic Law: Human Dignity and Freedom, where it belongs, more than in a law about Israel being a Jewish state.

Does Lauder believe that the administration of the late Yitzhak Rabin, which amended Basic Law: Human Dignity and Freedom without adding the magic word also tarnished Israel's equality?

However, the main target in Lauder's piece was "the Orthodox," who he paints with one brush, as if there are not huge differences within Israel's vibrant modern Orthodox, nationalist religious Zionist and haredi (ultra-Orthodox) communities.

Lauder refers to "Orthodoxy" as "a radical minority" and suggests that it alienates millions of Jews worldwide."

In truth, Orthodox Judaism is the fastest growing branch of our faith in the United States. While Reform synagogues are closing, and the Conservative movement is struggling to attract young people, Orthodox synagogues are full and expanding.

Perhaps Lauder should use his pulpit in America's top-read newspapers to fight against assimilation and intermarriage and ensure that America's other movements are as successful in invigorating their people as the Orthodox.

Far from "crushing the core of contemporary Jewish existence," when members of Israel's government encourage Orthodox traditions, they are carrying out policies supported by their people. Our Orthodox traditions have kept the Jewish people going for more than 3,000 years.

Orthodox politicians in Israel have expressed support for compromises, including Naftali Bennett, who heads the Orthodox Bayit Yehudi party and boasts that he built an egalitarian prayer site at the Western Wall, and Rabbi Ovadia Yosef, the late spiritual mentor of the Sephardi haredi Shas party, who endorsed and enabled the passage of the Oslo Accords that Lauder championed.

Lauder warned that if Israel continues its policies, future leaders of the West will become hostile or indifferent to the Jewish state. Such threats ring hollow, considering that after two decades of Israel being told it would be shunned if there is no diplomatic process with the Palestinians, Netanyahu is being warmly welcomed on six continents.

What Lauder gets right in his piece is his call for unity. Clearly, Israel needs solidarity as it enters its eighth decade of existence.

I agree that we must "stop sowing division among ourselves." I hope that in his next submission to the Times, Lauder will do just that.

The Jerusalem Post

The Jewish Nation-State Law outside politics

The Nation-State Law complements the existing laws and gives expression to the right of the Jewish people to national self-determination in Israel.

SEPTEMBER 12, 2018

In a fitting culmination to 5778, a year when Israel's Jewish Nation-State Law caused a greater uproar than any Israeli law in years, a group of seven Arab Knesset members visited the European Union in Brussels over the past week for meetings with top European officials.

They met with the ambassadors to the EU of every European country, members of the EU parliament, the foreign minister of Luxembourg, and the head of Israel's Joint Arab List, MK Ayman Odeh, met with European foreign policy chief Frederica Mogherini.

The results the Arab MKs scandalously sought were the condemnation of Israel – the country in whose parliament they serve – and increased pressure on Israel to have the law repealed.

By all accounts, the visit was a failure. The Arab MKs did not receive what they wanted. In fact, the official statement released by Mogherini's office shortly after Odeh left was a moral victory for Israel.

"The Nation-State Law is first and foremost a matter of how Israel chooses to define itself, and we fully respect the internal Israeli debate on this," Mogherini's office said.

This did not come from the talking points of Israel's Foreign Ministry or some pro-Israel pundit. When the European Union, which normally does not shy away from condemning Israel, releases a statement like that, it must be taken very seriously.

Mogherini must have done her homework. Indeed, the Nation-State Law was preceded by other Basic Laws and Supreme Court rulings that clearly establish the principles of democracy, the democratic structure of the state and the rights of the individual in the State of Israel.

The Nation-State Law complements the existing laws and gives expression to the right of the Jewish people to national self-determination in Israel.

In part because of pressure from international bodies like the EU, the United Nations and UNESCO in particular, there have been increasing attempts to question and deny the right of the Jewish people to its national homeland. In view of this situation, the Knesset drafted legislation making clear that Israel is the national home of the Jewish people.

New York Times columnist and former Jerusalem Post editor-in-chief Bret Stephens said it best when he wrote a column called "The Jewish Nation-State bill non-scandal.

"What the bill is not is the death of Israeli democracy," he wrote. "It was enacted democratically and can be overturned the same way. It is not the death of Israeli civil liberties – still guaranteed under the 1992 Basic Law on Human Dignity and Liberty and visibly reaffirmed by the large public protests following the bill's enactment.

AND IT IS not apartheid – a cheap slur from people whose grasp of the sinister mechanics of apartheid is as thin as their understanding of the complexities of Israeli politics."

The fact that Arab Knesset members called a press conference in Brussels, in which they called upon the world to condemn as apartheid a law they were able to vote against in the Israeli parliament, is especially ironic. Blacks could have only dreamed of serving in the apartheid South African parliament in its latter decades.

It was Jewish leaders and legal experts who led the fight against apartheid in South Africa, due to the morality of the Jewish people and the understanding Jews have of what it is like to be minorities in countries around the world for 1,878 years.

That feeling of what it is like to be a minority as a Jew in Europe, and seeing the antisemitism toward French Jewish artillery officer Alfred Dreyfus, compelled Theodore Herzl to write the book The Jewish State and to found the modern Zionist movement. In his book, Herzl wrote his vision of how politics in the Jewish state will protect minorities.

"Politics must take shape in the upper strata and work downward," Herzl wrote. "But no member of the Jewish state will be oppressed. Every man will be able and will wish to rise in it. Thus a great upward tendency will pass through our people; every individual by trying to raise himself, also raising the whole body of citizens. The ascent will take a moral form, useful to the state and serviceable to the national idea."

Protests against the Nation-State Law by Druze, which recently resumed, prove Herzl correct in hindsight. They are empowered by democracy in Israel.

They are working to build their power ahead of the forthcoming 2019 election in Israel by using the Jewish Nation-State Law, exactly as Prime Minister Benjamin Netanyahu has done, and there is nothing wrong with that.

The Arab MKs, by contrast, are crossing red lines by seeking the condemnation of their own country in key international forums. Their behavior reinforces more than ever why Israel needed to pass a Jewish Nation-State Law in order to protect itself.

Understanding the political context of the new law and the uproar over it is key. If the European Union understood that message, one can only hope that other frequent critics of Israel will too.
If that happens, 5779 will be a better and sweeter year.

The Jewish Press

What GA delegates should learn from Jack Nagel

OCTOBER 25, 2018

The Jewish Federations of North America will hold its annual General Assembly in Tel Aviv this week.

The event has been marketed under the slogan "Israel and the Diaspora: We need to talk." That slogan highlights the differences that divide Israelis and U.S. Jews.

Much has been written about that divide growing in recent years, for reasons ranging from politics to pluralism. Undoubtedly, there will be protests and acrimony regarding the venue and speakers.

But if GA delegates and their dissenters are looking for the antidote to the problem, they should look no further than the life of the great religious Zionist philanthropist Jack Nagel, who died last week, as he was approaching his 96th birthday.

Jack was a Holocaust survivor born in Poland who came to the United States in the late 1940s and married his eishet chayil Gitta after only a few weeks of courtship 63 years ago. Their union gave birth to four children, over a dozen grandchildren and more than 10 great-grandchildren.

Their descendants care deeply about the State of Israel and its future and are involved in Jewish and pro-Israel causes. Their children are active in charities from Israel Bonds to NORPAC, from Amit and Emunah to AIPAC, from YULA high school to fire departments and July 4 chamber of commerce parades.

Pursuing the American dream, Jack built a successful construction company that developed more than 2000 homes in the L.A. area and today is immersed in every aspect of the real estate business in California. But to many, he was mostly known for his philanthropy.

In the U.S., Jack and Gitta have helped support Yeshiva University, the Simon Wiesenthal Center and Jewish schools in LA, founding Yavneh Hebrew Academy. In Israel, they donated the Jewish Heritage Center at Bar-Ilan University in Ramat Gan and the Nagel Family Pediatric Pavilion at Shaare Zedek in Jerusalem. They were involved and honored by the many organizations his family is championing today. Jack and Gitta were awarded doctorates and certificates of recognition by a wide range of Jewish organizations.

Being a survivor inspired Jack to thrive and to give back. His entire family, except for one surviving sister, died during the Holocaust. He saw life as a gift, and he felt he clearly had a duty and responsibility to rebuild what was lost in Europe.

To that end, he was very involved in the Mizrachi World Movement, most particularly at the Religious Zionists of America, where he served as president for many years, spreading Torat Eretz Israel across the world and strengthening the bond between the international Jewish community and the State of Israel.

Jack was also always involved in the L.A. Jewish Federation and the United Jewish Appeal. He appreciated the greater Jewish community and the need to bring all Jews together, including both religious and secular.

He was a frequent visitor to Israel, coming last during the week of Yom Ha'atzmut, when Gitta was given a letter of distinction from Bar-Ilan. Despite his failing health, he considered leading the religious Zionist flag procession through Jerusalem.

For him, Israel was the place for Jews to live, and if not reside, then to support unquestionably.

Jack wasn't known for getting involved in politics. When others were divisive, he was always the one who tried to bring people together, insisting that the next generation continue to appreciate the importance of the strong US-Israel relationship.

In the final analysis, Jack Nagel was a man of righteousness and integrity. Those attributes can help the delegates to the GA focus on what is truly important: The continued unity of the Jewish people in Israel and around the world.

May the memory of Jack Nagel truly be for a blessing.

The Jerusalem Post

AIPAC must stay out of Israeli politics

Just like every commercial for medicine on TV and every package of cigarettes has a disclaimer, so do AIPAC events.

FEBRUARY 27, 2019

In the countless AIPAC events that I have attended over the years, I have always admired the long disclaimer of neutrality that is read at the start of the program.

Just like every commercial for medicine on TV and every package of cigarettes has a disclaimer, so do AIPAC events.

"AIPAC is the American-Israel Public Affairs Committee," the disclaimer starts. "AIPAC is not a PAC. We are neither Democrat nor Republican. We are neither Likud, nor Labor. We do not support any political party in Israel or the US."

This statement of neutrality is a really dull way to start an event, but it is actually the key to AIPAC's success. While other pro-Israel movements have come and gone, AIPAC has only gotten stronger, and the growing number of attendees at their annual National Policy Conference in Washington testifies to that.

In an age where TV news channels and newspapers no longer make an effort to hide their political bias, AIPAC's neutrality on internal US and Israeli politics has been absolutely refreshing. It also is exactly what is needed for Israel, whose bipartisan support on Capitol Hill and across the US is its top strategic asset.

That is why I was so dismayed to see AIPAC's response to Prime Minister Benjamin Netanyahu's successful move to encourage the religious Zionist Bayit Yehudi, National Union and Otzma Yehudit parties to run together in the April 9 Israeli elections.

"AIPAC has a long-standing policy not to meet with members of this racist and reprehensible party," the organization said of Otzma Yehudit.

The reason why AIPAC felt compelled to release this statement is that Otzma Yehudit is made up of disciples of the late Rabbi Meir Kahane, whose Kach party was deemed racist and outlawed by the Israeli High Court of Justice. While Rabbi Kahane must also be remembered for his positive work for encouraging aliyah from Russia, I also disagreed with his views on minorities.

As a proud religious Zionist, I believe that Israel has a religious obligation to treat its minorities well. Improving Israel's image around the world is necessary to ensure its future in a world in which the battles fought on social media are just as important as those fought on the military battlefield.

But I am not AIPAC. I don't have that disclaimer of neutrality stamped on me. And there are plenty of people like me who have political views. There is only one AIPAC.

We need AIPAC to have that neutrality in order to protect Israel from its critics on the extreme Left, extreme Right and everywhere in between.

The moment AIPAC puts itself on that map, it renders itself as irrelevant.

Those defending the AIPAC statement have said that it is no big deal, because they are just distancing themselves from a fringe party. But the world has not interpreted it that way.

Netanyahu's name was not in their tweet, but Otzma Yehudit would have had little of chance of crossing the 3.25% electoral threshold and entering the Knesset if Netanyahu did not pressure the heads of Bayit Yehudi and the National Union to give the party slots on their joint list. Netanyahu made the move in order to prevent the loss of thousands of right-wing votes that would have been thrown out.

Though it was obviously not intentional, AIPAC was seen as criticizing Netanyahu, the prime minister of Israel, and the Likud, the ruling party of Israel, which won a quarter of the Knesset seats in the 2015 election and current polls suggest that it will win at least that many this time around.

What kind of message does that send to the new members of Congress, the overwhelming majority of whom still have so much to learn about Israel and the Middle East?

I urge AIPAC to reconsider its decision to interfere in Israel's democratic election. After all, who knows better than AIPAC how important Israel's democracy is to the future of the Jewish state?

Perhaps the next time an AIPAC representative begins a parlor meeting, the disclaimer can say that AIPAC also stands for Avoiding Israeli Politics at All Costs.

The Jerusalem Post

Don't give up on the Democrats: The need for bipartisanship

The massacre of Jews at the Tree of Life Congregation in Pittsburgh in October, the most deadly attack on Jews in American history, was a painful reminder.

MARCH 15, 2019

In the Passover Seder next month, Jewish families around the world will recall how "In each and every generation, they rise up against us to destroy us, and the Holy One, blessed be He, rescues us from their hands."

That has unfortunately been historically accurate, since the days of Pharaoh, to the Babylonians, Haman, Greeks, Romans, Crusaders, expulsion from Western European countries, pogroms in Russia, the Holocaust and the repeated attempts to annihilate the State of Israel.

The massacre of Jews at the Tree of Life Congregation in Pittsburgh in October, the most deadly attack on Jews in American history, was a painful reminder that Jews are not entirely safe in the US now.

Especially following that attack, there can be no excuse for any public figure, certainly elected officials, to engage in any form of antisemitism. It should be obvious that just like there is zero tolerance in America for statements against women and the lesbian, gay, bisexual and transgender community, no antisemitism can be tolerated, accepted, or explained away as ignorance.

Therefore,the dual loyalty canard of freshman Minnesota Congresswoman Ilhan Omar was particularly offensive. The fact that she reaffirmed her statements even after her Democratic Congressional colleagues asked her to apologize proves Omar's offenses were intentional. Her remarks were designed to introduce antisemitism into the mainstream debate and to legitimize and foster that discussion.

In the final analysis, antisemitism is a disease that infects the antisemite. We may be the intended victims but the disease is theirs.

The Democratic leadership disappointed the Jewish community by not insisting on a Congressional resolution exclusively condemning antisemitism. This surrender to extremists in the party's progressive wing is a frightening omen for the future as that wing's power grows.

House Majority Whip Jim Clyburn made matters worse by suggesting that Omar had a "more personal" relationship to suffering than the descendants of Holocaust survivors. For a man whose job is to build a consensus among the new Democratic majority, he should have known better.

Nevertheless, the mainstream Democratic Party remains pro-Israel. The leadership remains in the hands of unquestionably pro-Israel Congressmen and not the likes of Omar, Rashida Tlaib or Alexandria Ocasio-Cortez.

There are 32 Jewish Democrats in the House and Senate whose efforts for American Jewry and for Israel cannot be underestimated, as well as Congressmen like Tom Suozzi who rightly condemned Omar:

"Antisemitism is real and growing," Suozzi told CNN. "After Representative Omar made apologies in the past for statements she made in the past and now made them again, we have to be very firm in clearly speaking out against antisemitism and say you can't do this. It's wrong to question people's loyalty because they're pro-Israel."

Suozzi said Omar's statements "conjure up the worst antisemitic stereotypes."

It is that mainstream Democratic Party that must be nurtured by the American Jewish leadership, so it doesn't get taken over by extremists and overt antisemites like Labour in Britain. Those advocating giving up on the Democrats have forgotten that Israel's bipartisan relationship is its top strategic asset.

While empowering that mainstream, it is important to keep fighting the fringes, so their views do not gradually become accepted. The best approach is that of AIPAC, which has been working sensitively to maintain support for Israel across the aisle, even when it has been dragged into the headlines.

"Charges of dual loyalty are antisemitic and insult millions of patriotic Americans – Jewish and non-Jewish – who stand by Israel," AIPAC courageously tweeted in response to Omar's attack. "Our alliance with Israel is in the US national interest. We will not be deterred from exercising our right to advocate for a strong US-Israel relationship."

It is that spirit that must unite the Jewish people in the face of challenges that are intensifying. Unity in the American Jewish community is more important now than ever, as is educating Jews so they appreciate their history and background. We need to eradicate ignorance among all Jews and especially young Jews.

Each individual can do his part, simply by learning more about Israel and Judaism. An important step toward achieving both that unity and an unequaled learning experience is attending this month's AIPAC Policy Conference.

As the Hebrew phrase goes regarding encountering obstacles: "We have overcome Pharaoh. We will overcome this, too." We must.

The Jerusalem Post

AIPAC: Balancing bipartisanship and being thankful

If we are commanded to be grateful and threatened so harshly if we are not, it is important to examine our individual behavior and that of the Jewish people as a whole.

APRIL 4, 2019

King Solomon provides an important lesson about the Jewish concept of gratitude, hakarat hatov, in the Book of Proverbs.

"Evil will never depart from the home of one who repays good with evil," Solomon wrote.
That verse is the ultimate statement of God's commitment to a just world and the ultimate challenge to humanity in general and the Jewish people in particular.

If we are commanded to be grateful and threatened so harshly if we are not, it is important to examine our individual behavior and that of the Jewish people as a whole.

This is true when it comes to politics in Washington, especially last week, when some 18,000 Jews gathered in the capital for the annual AIPAC Policy Conference to demonstrate their unwavering support for Israel.

Attending this year's conference, it is clear that many of the attendees are facing moral and strategic dilemmas due to the nuances of American and Israeli political realities.

Even the harshest critics of President Donald Trump admit that what he has done for Israel over the past two and a half years is extraordinary and unequaled.

Moving the American Embassy to Jerusalem, breaking the nuclear deal with Iran, fighting for Israel at the United Nations and now recognizing Israeli sovereignty over the Golan Heights are foremost among his game-changing steps that must be appreciated.

The people who aren't showing gratitude to Trump have good reasons. They believe he has not done enough to stop the rhetoric that they believe has led to antisemitism, like the horrible massacre at Pittsburgh's Tree of Life Congregation.

Many are not able to compartmentalize their support for Trump's Israel's policies if they are disgusted by his policies on other issues that they care about and by Trump's personal behavior.

Some of them even say we should not applaud the steps the president has taken too loudly, because it could alienate his Democratic opponents. After all, bipartisanship is Israel's top strategic asset.

That attitude goes against what Solomon wrote.

The truth is that even Israel advocates who despise President Trump have an obligation to thank him loud and clear. A true friend of Israel would not silence our gratitude.

The people who oppose bipartisanship also have good reasons. They believe the Democrats haven't done enough to distance and discipline the antisemites in their party. The Democratic candidates who gave into pressure to not attend the policy conference reinforced those legitimate fears.

There are also those on the Republican side who think bipartisanship is no longer necessary, because Trump and others in his party are so pro-Israel when compared with Democratic presidential contenders who have only unfairly criticized Israel and allowed antisemitism to raise its ugly head unchecked.

But that also goes against Proverbs.

Bipartisanship has served Israel well for decades. A true friend of Israel would not suggest giving it up.

The needs for bipartisanship and gratitude do not cancel each other out. They go hand in hand, even at a time of severe polarization in America and in Israel.

This delicate balancing act between gratitude and bipartisanship is definitely a challenge, but it is a welcome one. It is so much better than what Jewish communities around the world have endured for centuries, with little to be thankful for and no party to cheer for.

Showing gratitude for Israel's bipartisan relationship with Washington is a good way of fulfilling Solomon's advice that good will be repaid with more good.

May the State of Israel be the kind of home for the Jewish people that avoids all evil and merits true goodness, justice and peace. May we always be relentless and unified in that effort.

The Jerusalem Post

Israel's election message to the world

The majority decided that they wanted Netanyahu to remain prime minister and the Center-Right to remain in power.

APRIL 12, 2019

Two days before Israelis went to the polls on Tuesday, Democratic presidential candidate Beto O'Rourke cast his ballot in the Israeli election.

He declared Prime Minister Benjamin Netanyahu a racist against Arabs and said he did not believe Netanyahu "represents the true will of the Israeli people" or the "best interests" of the relationship between the US and Israel.

The people of Israel then decided on their own what their true will is and what their best interests are.

The majority decided that they wanted Netanyahu to remain prime minister and the Center-Right to remain in power.

This undoubtedly upset O'Rourke and others, who believe that being a friend of Israel requires lecturing Israelis and telling them what they ought to believe.

Once upon a time, that might have worked. Israelis used to be more intimidated by the international community.

When Bill Clinton tried to dictate the terms of a Middle East peace agreement, most Israelis went along with it and gave him a chance. When he fought with Netanyahu, polls found that Israelis believed that the leader of the free world must be right.

But during the Obama administration, when there were disputes with Netanyahu, polls found that Israelis repeatedly took their prime minister's side. This election showed that Israelis aren't willing to go back to the way it used to be.

Blue and White heads Benny Gantz and Yair Lapid told The Jerusalem Post in interviews that they hoped US President Donald Trump and Russian President Vladimir Putin weren't interfering in the election on Netanyahu's behalf and that other world leaders desperately wanted Netanyahu to go.

But who are these world leaders? And why didn't they want Netanyahu to stay in power? Israelis evidently knew their motives enough to decide to disregard them.

Israelis chose to say no to the likes of the European Union, the United Nations and Beto, and instead side with their true friends like Trump.

They no longer feel pressured to make concessions that could harm their security and result in them losing control over land promised to the Jewish people by God in the Bible and won in a war of defense.

They appreciate what Trump has done in recognizing Jerusalem as Israel's capital, moving the US Embassy there, leaving the Iran nuclear deal, recognizing Israel's sovereignty over the Golan Heights, slightly changing the anti-Israel atmosphere at the UN and many other gifts to the Jewish state.

They also felt gratitude to Putin, who assisted in the long-awaited return of the body of missing-in-action soldier Zachary Baumel after 37 years for a proper burial in Israel.
Rewarding Trump and Putin for treating them well is only natural. So is ignoring the world leaders who did not really have Israel's best interests at heart.

Next Friday night, Jews in Israel and around the world will recall at their Passover Seder that in each and every generation, there have been world leaders who rose up to try to destroy our people.

Sometimes, it has been blatantly obvious, like in the Holocaust and the story of Purim. At other times, that attempt to harm the Jewish people was more subtle, even cloaked in claims of friendship.

But the Holy One, blessed be He, has rescued us from their hands.

This election has proven that the Jewish people in Israel are ready to tell the world that they no longer want to get to the point where God has to save them.

Israelis' will is to continue to succeed and thrive, and to determine their best interests on their own. Sending that message to the world on Election Day should be celebrated, as the Jewish Festival of Freedom approaches.

The Jerusalem Post

On the blessings of bifurcation

Around the time of Independence Day every year, the Pew Research Center conducts a survey that reveals good news for Israel.

MAY 9, 2019

Around the time of Independence Day every year, the Pew Research Center conducts a survey that reveals good news for Israel.

The annual survey asks Americans what they think about the people of Israel. As in years past, this year's poll of 10,523 American adults had very positive results.

Sixty-four percent of Americans view the Israeli people favorably, and only 28% view them unfavorably. This would be a cause for celebration were it not for the survey's follow-up question about the Israeli government.

With that question, the positive views go down from 64% to 41%, and the negative goes up from 28% to 51%. More than half of Americans have a negative opinion of the government the people of Israel chose in the April 9 election.

These numbers have caused alarm among some Jewish organizations in America. They have turned to Israelis and warned them to stop making choices that turn off Americans in general and young, "progressive" US Jews in particular.

However well-meaning, it is time for those alarm bells to stop.

As in any democracy, the people of Israel have a right to be governed by whomever they choose. They have repeatedly elected Prime Minister Benjamin Netanyahu and the Right, and it is not the place of people who do not live among Israelis to scold them.

Israelis have endured conventional warfare, hijackings, kidnappings, suicide bombings, shootings, stabbings, rockets, mortars, terror tunnels and now incendiary kites and balloons.

After all that, no one can blame them for not expecting white doves to be the next thing they see flying through the air.

The prospects for peace with the Palestinians have never been less of a priority than when Israelis went to vote. The politicians did not even talk about the issue, and journalists did not ask them about it.

It might be a top priority among left-wing American Jews in New York and California, but they have no right to impose their interests on the people of Israel in Sderot and Kiryat Shmona.

Those same left-wing American Jews care about the Western Wall deal, the advancement of non-Orthodox streams in Israel, the Women of the Wall and the increased power of haredim (ultra-Orthodox).
That is not what Israelis care about, and that is not a problem.

Israelis care about their security, about housing, about making ends meet and about the makeup of their society. They can vote for whatever party they believe will best alleviate their concerns.

The overwhelming majority of Israelis who are not Orthodox do not define themselves as secular, and very few of them align with one of the American non-Orthodox streams. They define themselves as traditional and are very respectful of their Jewish traditions, whatever their current level of religious observance.

While Israelis are moving more to the Right, non-Orthodox American Jews vote more to the Left. That is also not a problem.

American Jews across the political and religious spectra have a right to their opinions, and to vote for whichever candidates they choose.

It is only natural that people living in different places with different concerns will move in different directions. This bifurcation is healthy, not problematic.

The problems begin when Jews on one side of the Atlantic try to dictate to Jews on the other side what to think, how to feel and who to cast their ballots for.

They have a right to worry about each other. After all, that is what we Jews do. As the Talmud states, Kol Yisrael arevim ze lazeh, "All Jews are responsible for one another."

But neither side should try to take the upper hand over the other.

Instead, both sides should embrace the other in their arms, despite their many differences.

The Jerusalem Post

If you will Trump's plan, it is no dream

Every US president who has presented a peace plan has failed miserably. Then again, this plan, like the president, will be different from all of its predecessors.

MAY 25, 2019

Zionist visionary Theodor Herzl wrote in his utopian novel *Old New Land* that when it came to the establishment of a Jewish national home in the Land of Israel, "If you will it, it is no dream."

The book was published in 1902, 46 years before the founding of the State of Israel, when centuries of dreams of Jews around the world came true.

The impressive successes of Israel over the past 71 years undoubtedly surpass the state's founders' wildest dreams.

But Israel has never enjoyed a moment of true peace, and has been under the microscope of the overly critical international community from day one.

After decades of pressure from the world to make concessions that would endanger Israel's future, it is understandable that there are those who would doubt that a foreign leader would take genuine steps to improve Israel's security.

But President Donald Trump has consistently proven himself to be different from all of his predecessors and all other leaders around the world, so the peace plan he is expected to announce soon should neither be doubted nor dismissed.

When Republican Jewish Coalition chairman Norm Coleman recounted President Trump's help for Israel at the RJC conference in Las Vegas last month, he did so in a new version of the Passover song "Dayenu."

And indeed, every single monumental step the president made for Israel must be appreciated and celebrated.

Last week, Israel marked the first anniversary of the move of the American Embassy from Tel Aviv to Jerusalem. American administrations promised that step for 25 years before Trump, resisting tremendous pressure, implemented it.

US Ambassador to Israel David Friedman completed the implementation of the Jerusalem Embassy Act last week when he officially moved his residence to Israel's capital, which America recognized in December 2017.

By breaking the world's unfortunate deal with Iran, President Trump ensured Israel's continued existence. His sanctions on Iran are helpful, as were his decisions to declare Iran's Revolutionary Guard a terrorist group and to target funding for the Iranian-backed Hezbollah terrorists.

The Trump decision about the Middle East that faced the most justified criticism was his announcement last December about removing all American forces from Syria. But the US will be staying in Syria, which earned the praise of Israeli Ambassador to the US Ron Dermer at the AIPAC Policy Conference.

"Those soldiers have done a fantastic job at preventing Iran from simply rushing through this whole region with arms and weapons," he said, adding that the Trump administration's recognition of Israeli sovereignty over the Golan Heights "sends a very strong message to the enemies of Israel and to the people of Israel that America stands with Israel." When the Jewish state has been attacked by Hamas and Islamic Jihad, the Trump administration has defended and enabled Israel's right to self-defense. Even the atmosphere at the United Nations has finally changed for the better.

President Trump has proven himself worthy of the trust of Americans, whose economy has improved since he entered office. He is very transparent and does not lie.

Despite all of that, a Middle East peace plan obviously remains an ambitious endeavor. After all, every American president who has presented a plan for the Middle East has failed miserably.

Then again, even though it has not been released yet, it is clear that this plan, like the president, will be different from all of its predecessors.

It is new and creative. It does not reward Palestinian rejectionism.

It acknowledges that those who call themselves Palestinian are far from cohesive and are far from being a nation. They are many different tribes who have united solely out of hatred for Israel.

The plan is expected to give more control to local leaders of hamulot, or tribes. The significant differences between the Arabs of the West Bank and the Gaza Strip will be acknowledged, and both will be greatly assisted economically.

Importantly, the plan is set to call for the evacuation of no one from their home, and the entire basis of discussion about the Jews who settled their biblical homeland in Judea and Samaria will change.

US Secretary of State Mike Pompeo hinted to the Senate last month that the plan would not call for a two-state solution, saying that "the old set of ideas aren't worth retreading." Because most analysts think peace in the short term is not possible, it is time to ditch the two-state solution as a means of achieving a lasting peace.

US Special Envoy Jason Greenblatt has said repeatedly that the plan will focus on ensuring Israeli security, which is a welcome development after suicide bombers, shootings, stabbings, car rammings, terror tunnels, rockets, mortars, kites and other incendiary devices.

The regional approach to solving the conflict can be beneficial for both Israel and for Arab countries which can benefit from the Jewish state's innovation and economic prosperity. Countries weaning themselves off their dependency on oil can learn how Israel made the desert bloom.

It may all sound like a dream now, but Herzl was also doubted.

If this plan is willed – and it should be – it is no dream.

The Algemeiner

25 years of Iran, Argentina, and terrorism

JUNE 24, 2019

Next month will mark the 25th anniversary of the bombing of the AMIA building in Buenos Aires, which took the lives of 85 people and injured more than 300. The attack on the social services hub of the Argentine Jewish community remains the largest terrorist attack in Latin America. To this day, justice has not been served to the victims and their families.

For three years after the attack, the judge heading the inquiry produced 22 arrests — mostly Buenos Aires provincial policemen — and a trial that, in the end, amounted to nothing more than a diversionary wild goose chase. A representative of our organization attended every day of the nearly three-year trial.

The stench of a cover-up hovered over those proceedings. Not guilty verdicts were handed down for those brought to trial, and the judge was later impeached for attempting to bribe a witness to give testimony incriminating police officers and for his general mishandling of the case. He was summarily removed from his post.

What did come out of the scrutiny of the attack was the unmistakable hand of the Iranian regime. At first, it was studied speculation, but by 2006, two prosecutors in the case officially fingered Tehran. Operatives connected to the Iranian embassy in Buenos Aires were identified, but at that point, they all had made their way out of the country.

The case was turned over to two new prosecutors, Alberto Nisman and Marcelo Martínez Burgos, who in 2007 brought the matter to Interpol. They had requested that "red notices," or arrest warrants, be issued for nine suspects, including former Iranian president Ali Rafsanjani, former Iranian foreign minister Ali Akbar Velayati, and former Iranian ambassador to Argentina Hadi Soleimanpour. Interpol's executive committee let those three officials off the hook, choosing instead to issue notices for the other six suspects.

Years passed, but Nisman, now working alone, pressed ahead. In 2015, he was ready to release evidence that a deal had been negotiated at the highest levels of the two governments, which would see Tehran deliver oil to Argentina in exchange for food, weapons, and a pledge to convince Interpol to drop the red notices on the terrorist suspects.

On the eve of this information being shared in the Argentine Congress, Nisman was found dead in what the authorities called a suicide. Doubt immediately surfaced, given the nature of the charges Nisman was about to bring. Subsequently, the mysterious circumstances of Nisman's death have become clarified, and evidence points to him having been murdered.

The AMIA case is only one in a litany of terrorist acts carried out on foreign soil by the Iranian regime.

In 1992, foreshadowing the attack on the AMIA building two years later, a suicide bomber attacked the Israeli embassy in Buenos Aires, killing 29 and injuring 242. Responsibility was claimed by the Islamic Jihad organization, a group believed to have ties to Iran's Lebanese proxy Hezbollah.

Also that year, three Iranian opposition leaders and their translator were killed at the Mykonos restaurant in Berlin. The verdict in that case pointed to Iran's highest officials — as in the case in the AMIA bombing — having signed off on the attack. In 1996, in an attack on the Khobar Towers housing complex in Saudi Arabia, a truck bomb killed 19 American soldiers and a Saudi citizen, and nearly 500 people were injured. While credit was not claimed, it is widely believed that Hezbollah was behind the attack.

Iran's malign behavior operates on three fronts: its pursuit of nuclear weapons; its support for and use of terrorist proxies in the Middle East and beyond; and its serial abuse of human rights of women, adherents of the Baha'i faith, political dissenters, juvenile offenders, and the LGBTQ community.
The Trump administration has rightly pointed to serious omissions in the Joint Comprehensive Plan of Action (JCPOA), the multilateral agreement meant to curb Iran's nuclear program. But in bringing Iran to

the table, the international community made a monumental error in judgment in not opening talks at the same time on the other two legs of Tehran's destructive behavior. Had it done so, we might well have been able to shine a conclusive light on the activities of its agents in Buenos Aires on July 18, 1994.

Today, at the site of the AMIA bombing, there is a stunning memorial to those killed on that day 25 years ago, created by the Israeli artist Yaakov Agam. Perhaps more touching are the names of the victims listed at the site: professionals of Jewish organizations, office workers, and people from the community who had come to seek assistance for one or another personal or family matter. A van packed with 600 pounds of explosives put an end to all of that, in seconds.

The Iranians are still at it. They've provided Hezbollah with more than 100,000 rockets, and Hamas with many thousands. They work with the likes of Hugo Chavez and Nicolás Maduro's Venezuela, and with North Korea. They have taken over Lebanon, have ensconced themselves in Syria, and are meddling in Iraq, Yemen, and the Eastern Mediterranean.

Tehran has used the JCPOA as cover for its other nefarious activities. It has enjoyed impunity for far too long. Its decades-long record of promoting terrorism to advance its hegemonic objectives demands accountability and international opprobrium. That the European Union could not agree on designating Hezbollah a terrorist organization (it ultimately created the fiction of military and political "wings" of the organization so it could have it both ways) speaks to the failure of international will to confront the Iranian menace.

In the meantime, a quarter century has passed without the perpetrators of the AMIA bombing and their sponsor being brought to account. For the sake of the victims and their families, is it too much to ask that justice be served? If we are to turn the tide on state sponsored terrorism, let it begin here — before the dust collects on memory while those who were responsible remain free.

The Jerusalem Post

Give pressuring the Palestinians a chance

Obama's plans put undue pressure on Israel, America's closest ally. His policies granted massive amounts of financial support to Iran, America's greatest enemy.

JULY 13, 2019

When Barack Obama was president of the United States, too many Americans, especially American Jews, adopted his policies and plans blindly.

Obama's plans put undue pressure on Israel, America's closest ally. His policies granted massive amounts of financial support to Iran, America's greatest enemy.

But in the eyes of Obama's supporters, this was all kosher, because it came from a man who could seemingly walk on water.

Now that Donald Trump is president of the United States, this has all been reversed.

It does not matter how correct his policies and plans might be. Too many Americans, especially American Jews, will oppose them blindly.

The same people who supported Obama's awful deal with Iran, just because it had his name on it, will automatically oppose Trump's plans for the Middle East, no matter how creative, fresh, properly researched and well-thought out.

Blindly ruling out Trump's plans is illogical, because from what is known of them, they are very different from all other Middle East peace plans in the past. All those plans have failed pathetically, so Trump's plan being different should give it more of a chance of success.

The premise of past plans has been to pressure the party in the region perceived to be stronger, Israel, to make serious concessions, while letting the Palestinians pay not much more than lip service. The worst example was Obama's plan, in which borders would be decided at the beginning and the refugee issue at the end, meaning Israel gives up its territory and security first, in hopes that the Palestinians will later concede their desire to flood Israel with Arabs until it is no longer a Jewish state.

Trump's plan remains unpublished except for its economic components. But it is clear that it will call for unprecedented pressure on the Palestinians.

This, unsurprisingly, has those who worked on past plans up in arms. David Makovsky, who directs the Project on Arab-Israel Relations at the Washington Institute for Near East Policy, wrote an op-ed in The Washington Post criticizing the economic plan revealed by Trump's senior adviser Jared Kushner at the conference in Bahrain, which Makovksky attended as an observer.

"The Trump administration and its critics share a common all-or-nothing approach to the Middle East, and when it's all-or-nothing in the Middle East, it's nothing," Makovsky wrote. "There is a reason that Kushner cannot veer from the straitjacket of the all-or-nothing approach, which has been tried at least three times before in Israeli-Palestinian relations and failed repeatedly. The Trump administration's method in this conflict, as it is to others, is to apply maximal pressure: You get nothing unless you agree to their deal."

Makovsky wrote that Kushner should have instead suggested a few immediately achievable steps, no-strings-attached, such as economic projects for the Palestinians, but decided against it.

"The White House's inflexible approach means that if the final-status ideas offered by the political portion of the plan don't gain support, the economic package goes down the tubes," he lamented. "The linkage is almost certainly doomed."

No, David Makovsky. It is all the previous attempts to advance the diplomatic process in the Middle East that were doomed, because they did not put the pressure on the Palestinians that is needed to succeed. Giving the Palestinians a free pass for continuing to reject or violate every agreement proposed clearly did not work.

The linkage proposed by Kushner ensures that the Palestinians will no longer be left off the hook for their intransigence. From now on, they will be held accountable for their misdeeds, just like Israel and other states in conflicts around the world.

Just like Trump promised when he ran for president, his administration is asking for success to be given a chance when it comes to Middle East peacemaking. After success was not achieved by pressuring Israel, isn't pressuring the Palestinians worth trying?

Such policies should give those who want a brighter day for the Palestinians and the Israelis new hope.

They should seek that hope. Even if it comes from Donald Trump.

The Jerusalem Post

The double-edged sword of Omar and Tlaib

Perhaps ignoring the visit of the congresswomen and waiting patiently for the world to forget about the visit of these fringe politicians would have been the right thing to do.

AUGUST 19, 2019

In 609 BCE, Josiah, the young king of Judea, made a fateful decision about whether to let an Egyptian army pass through his borders – which ultimately led to his death and the Babylonian Exile.

Although 2,028 years have passed, deciding who can enter the Jewish state remains a challenging question. Prime Minister Benjamin Netanyahu was put in a difficult situation by the pending visit of US congresswomen Rashida Tlaib and Ilhan Omar, which presented him with a double-edged sword.

On the one hand, Netanyahu did not want to play into their hands and prove their charges that Israel limits democracy and has something to hide. He certainly did not want to cause problems for American Jewish organizations or risk Israel's bipartisan relationship with the United States.

Perhaps ignoring the visit of the congresswomen and waiting patiently for the world to forget about the visit of these fringe politicians would have been the right thing to do.

On the other hand, these women are declared antisemites, who were up to no good. Their itinerary contained no meetings with any Israelis. Even if they have tough questions for Israel, they were not looking for answers but simply to embarrass and humiliate the Jewish state.

Congresswomen Tlaib and Omar are nothing like their more than 70 Democratic and Republican colleagues who have visited over the past three weeks and met with both Netanyahu and Palestinian chief negotiator Saeb Erekat.

The United States also has limits on who can enter the country, choosing to deny the entry of then-MK Michael Ben-Ari in 2012. Supreme Court Justice Oliver Wendell Holmes Jr. wrote a century ago that free speech in the US does not include falsely shouting fire in a theater and causing a panic.

Every democracy would take steps against those who want to destroy it. The BDS movement that the congresswomens' trip was set to advance wants to destroy the State of Israel. The trip was set to be co-sponsored by Miftah, a Ramallah-based organization, whose leaders not only back BDS but have expressed sympathy for suicide bombers.

The most controversial reason not to let in Tlaib and Omar was that US President Donald Trump asked Netanyahu not to do so and tweeted that letting them in would show weakness. The prime minister obviously cannot afford to be seen as weak with an election ahead, and this president has done so much for Israel that his requests, reasonable or not, should not be ignored.

It could be argued that Trump's motives are impure and Netanyahu harmed Israel by letting the president use him to paint the Democratic Party in the extremist image of Tlaib and Omar. But if that is what it takes for Trump to be reelected, despite his fickle behavior on both the Middle East and the economy, that is clearly in Israel's interest, because no potential opponent would do for Israel what Trump has done. For all those reasons, AIPAC's decision to give legitimacy to Israel's critics by scolding Israel for not permitting Tlaib and Omar into the country was incorrect, even though it was understandable.

Furthermore, AIPAC is supposed to follow the lead from Israel: Israel is not supposed to follow the lead from AIPAC. In the final analysis, Israel does not need to aid the enemy in the name of bipartisanship, and a Congressional badge is not a shield for antisemitism. Facing that double-edged sword, Netanyahu made the right decision. The result should be that, unlike the negative future brought by Josiah's decision, Netanyahu's should enable Israel to continue to thrive.

The Jerusalem Post

Why Tzom Gedalia's lesson of unity applies now

There are those who see compromise as surrender, weakness, defeat. They could not be further from the truth.

OCTOBER 1, 2019

Wednesday marks the 2,600th anniversary of the tragic murder of Gedelia Ben Ahikam, the governor of Judea, by a Jewish assassin named Ishmael Ben Netanya.

The murder, which ended Jewish self rule until Israel was founded, is marked by a minor fast. But its message is anything but minor. Tzom Gedalia has been increasingly marked as a kind of Jewish unity day, as an antidote to the assassination.

That message resonates more than ever now, with unity talks going on among Israel's politicians to form a new government and end the political stalemate in the modern Jewish state. Political compromise seems more elusive than ever and more essential than ever for our future.

There are those who see compromise as surrender, weakness, defeat. They could not be further from the truth.

If handled properly, compromise can reinforce ideology, strength and victory. That is what should be done now in the coalition talks that are just getting started.

Every party should be able to stick to principles if they have them. It is a pity that not too many parties have them anymore.

The Likud has not published a platform on key issues in Israel in 20 years, Blue and White does have a platform. They even translated it into English. But most people think it has on it only three words: Anyone but Bibi.

The party that called itself Yamina in the election spoke very firmly against joining a government led by Blue and White leader Benny Gantz, Now, its leaders are practically begging to enter his coalition.

This raises the need for parties to have a manifesto explaining their views to Israel and to the world. They can then stick with the platform or explain that they prioritized one aspect of their beliefs over another to take the practical step of implementing some of their policies in the government.

If platforms were more clear, taking steps that were far away from what a party believes in would be harder to sell to their constituency and would likely not be attempted.

Wanting to be part of the governing coalition should be seen as acceptable for any party. The political horse trading that takes place to build a coalition is perfectly normal and should not be a matter for criticism.

At the time of this writing, President Reuven Rivlin has asked Prime Minister Benjamin Netanyahu to form a government, but chances are seen as very low that he will succeed. Centrist and left-wing parties are refusing to join a government led by him.

These parties should look at the current moment from a historical perspective and keep in mind that the most important goal right now needs to be reuniting the people after months of political turmoil.

Rivlin rightfully called upon all the parties to stop disqualifying each other. Bereaved mother Miriam Peretz, who lost two sons in battle and was wooed unsuccessfully by many parties, made an impassioned plea for a unity government.

Yamina's leaders expressed willingness to join a broad unity government if it was led by Blue and White leader Benny Gantz. The parties in the Center and Center-Left should be saying the same about a government led by Netanyahu.

It would send a powerful message to Israel's allies and enemies around the world if Netanyahu and then Gantz rotated as prime minister and governed together. It would distance Israel from the political messes in the United States, United Kingdom and Spain and let the healing begin.

What better day to start that healing than Tzom Gedalia, our national day of unity – the day where Israel tells the world that our Jewish state will never self-destruct again.

The Jerusalem Post

Israeli politicians and the sin of foolishness

Many politicians have what to apologize for, and there's no time like the days after Yom Kippur.

OCTOBER 18, 2019

Jews around the world recently pounded their chests at Yom Kippur services as they said, "For the sin we have sinned before you through foolish speech."

There is no time like the days after Yom Kippur to repent over the sins of statements that should have never been made. It is said that the heavenly doors to repentance only close on Hoshana Raba, the final day of Hol Hamoed Sukkot, the intermediate days of the festival.

This need for repentance is especially true for politicians, whose words resonate around the world. One of the lessons of the fall holidays is the power and impact of words.

As Herb Keinon pointed out on the pages of this newspaper, Foreign Minister Israel Katz triggered a diplomatic crisis with Poland by quoting former prime minister Yitzhak Shamir saying that Poles imbibe antisemitism with their mother's milk.

Katz still has not apologized for that statement, which insulted a country with 38 million people in the aftermath of a since-revoked law in Poland that said anyone who accuses the nation of complicity during the Holocaust could be handed a prison sentence of up to three years.

I had an opportunity to meet President of Poland Andrzej Duda recently, and he said he was upset that Katz had not apologized. I told him I have gratitude to Poland, because a righteous couple risked their lives and the lives of their three children by hiding my parents for four years through the Holocaust.

I owe my very existence to these people. Our family is still in touch with them.

While my family did not want to go back to Poland because antisemitism is still part of life there, there are many righteous Poles and their descendants, and it is absolutely wrong to judge all of them together. Duda himself said he knows his people are not perfect. No nation has among its people only heroes or altruists.

But Katz should see that it is time to move forward and heal.

He is far from the only Israeli politician who needs to repent. Former education and Diaspora affairs minister Naftali Bennett, who had an awful 5779 in Israeli politics, has a bad habit of also dabbling in the politics of the United States.

Following US President Donald Trump's questionable decision to withdraw American forces from Syria, Bennett decided to react on Twitter in English.

"At this time, we, Israelis, pray for the Kurd People who are under a brutal Turkish attack," Bennett wrote, mistakes left unchanged. "The lesson for Israel is simple: Israel will ALWAYS defend itself by itself. The Jewish State will never put its fate in the hands of others, including our great friend, the USA."

While every word Bennett wrote is correct, what point is there in a leading Israeli politician insulting the American administration on social media? Prime Minister Benjamin Netanyahu, whose foreign policy experience dwarfs every other living Israeli politician, was much more careful and waited for the right time to tweet on the issue.

This is not the first time Bennett made the mistake of interfering in American politics in a manner worthy of special chest-beating at Bennett's synagogue in Ra'anana.

Then there are the statements about matters of religion and state from both secular and haredi (ultra-Orthodox) politicians that did nothing to calm tensions and bring either side closer to the other's point of view. Blue and White leader Benny Gantz's campaign against "extortionist" haredim was no more acceptable than the most extreme statements against secular people and left-wingers of the Noam Party.

The final chest-beatings should go to Democratic Union MK Yair Golan and other politicians across the Israeli political spectrum who have compared virtually anyone to Nazis.

It is not the 1940s, thank God. We have a Jewish state to protect the Jewish people.

Now all we need is to stop ourselves from making statements that make us into our own worst enemies.

The Jerusalem Post

A policy change of biblical proportions

The world must realize that the Land of Israel is ours.

NOVEMBER 14, 2019

Biblical commentator Rashi's first comment on the Torah is that the reason why Genesis began with the creation of the world and not the first commandment was to teach that the Jewish people have a God-given right to the Land of Israel.

The more than eight centuries since Rashi wrote his commentary have proven how necessary it was for the Bible to begin by making that point.

Since then, the connection of the Jewish people to its land has been continuously questioned. That has been especially true over the past 50 years regarding cities highlighted in Genesis, such as Hebron, Nablus, Bethlehem – and of course, Jerusalem.

That is why US Secretary of State Mike Pompeo's statement about the legality of so-called settlements was a policy change of biblical proportions.

"The establishment of Israeli civilian settlements in the West Bank is not per se inconsistent with international law," Pompeo said.

As an attorney, I can say that Pompeo's statement is legally correct. As George Mason University law professor Eugene Kontorovich wrote: "Under international law, occupation occurs when a country takes over the sovereign territory of another country. But the West Bank was never part of Jordan, which seized it in 1949 and ethnically cleansed its entire Jewish population. Nor was it ever the site of an Arab Palestinian state."

As a religious Zionist, our ideology is strengthened by seeing the leaders of the world confirm that our land belongs to us. The midrash, which talks about an oath of the Jewish people to not forcefully reclaim our land without the world's permission, is once again rendered obsolete.

Pompeo's statement about Judea and Samaria, like US President Donald Trump's December 2017 recognition of Jerusalem as Israel's capital, belongs in the same league as the Balfour Declaration a century earlier, when the world's leading empire affirmed the right for a Jewish homeland in the Land of Israel.

The Balfour Declaration led three years later to the San Remo Conference, where the world adopted the declaration's call for a Jewish state in the Land of Israel. If only Secretary Pompeo's words about Judea and Samaria would have faced similar international affirmation rather than the condemnation they received!

Instead, it was condemned by European countries, who deny the reality of Jews living in Judea and Samaria for 3,300 out of the last 3,500 years. While they can choose to label selectively, they will never change our history.
Abraham, Isaac and Jacob walked those hills, and they will remain part of Israel forever.

Pompeo also deserves praise for saying that the policy which says that Israel's establishment of civilian settlements is inconsistent with international law has not worked and has not advanced the cause of peace.

This has been proven time and time again. Israel withdrew from every settlement in the Gaza Strip and has received tens of thousands of rockets in return, but no peace.

Trump's predecessor, Barack Obama, spent eight years obsessing over settlements. But the only negotiations between Israel and the Palestinians during his tenure took place during the nine months starting in July 2013, when his administration agreed to ignore construction in Judea and Samaria.

Obama's experience proved that what sets back peace is not where a Jew lives but those who are obsessed over where he lives.

His parting efforts to get Israel condemned in the United Nations for settlement construction indicated that Obama never got over that obsession.

Now that America's policies are completely different, it is time for Europe and the rest of the world to follow suit, even left-wingers in Israel. Pro-Israel groups operating in the US dare not equivocate in their thanks and support, or obfuscate their position in confusing tweets.

There was no thievery. As Rashi says: The world must realize that the Land of Israel is ours.

The Jerusalem Post

Reaping rewards for remarkable courage

Why American Jewish organizations must appreciate President Trump's peace plan.

JANUARY 31, 2020

President Donald Trump had already proven that he was an unprecedented friend of Israel when he recognized Jerusalem as Israel's capital, moved the US Embassy there, recognized Israeli sovereignty over the Golan Heights and broke the world's bad deal with Iran.

But the step he took on Tuesday when he unveiled the "Deal of the Century" not only trumps everything the president did for Israel before, it surpasses any step taken by any international leader for the Jewish people over the past 100 years. I was proud to be in the audience when the president spoke brilliantly.

The Balfour Declaration of 1917, the San Remo Conference of 1920, the UN Partition Plan of 1947 and recognition of the new State of Israel in 1948 were all extremely important historic steps that must not be taken for granted.

But following all those steps and the initiation of all prior peace processes, Israel still relied on the good graces of the international community, and in some cases also on its neighbors who wanted to push the Jews into the Sea.

This time it is different. President Trump's plan depends on Israel and only Israel taking action to implement it. Israel can immediately start applying Israeli law to the lands where the Jews of Judea and Samaria live.

After decades of uncertainty about where Jews can build in an unprovoked and uncensured manner, Israel will be able to expand from

Jerusalem and Tel Aviv eastward without any problems, and build seamlessly and contiguously.

The world is largely unaware, but the main complaint of the average Israeli for decades has been a housing crisis in the center of pre-1967 Israel that has raised the cost of living to a level that has made it hard for young families to make ends meet.

This plan would resolve that problem very quickly, because construction to expand Israel's population centers could begin right away, unhindered by the world's pretensions of morality and incorrect definitions of international law.

Existing communities and blocs in Judea and Samaria would finally be recognized and legitimized. New large blocks will be created. No Jews or Arabs will be uprooted from their homes.

Maintaining Israeli security, which was a challenge in previous plans proposed by the United States, is no longer an issue here, because the IDF would maintain security control and protect both Israel and the entrances to where the Palestinians would continue to live.

The plan gives the Palestinians four years to come to the table but no longer relies on them. They are being asked to renounce terrorism, stop funding terrorism, demilitarize Gaza, recognize Jerusalem as Israel's capital and stop trying to get Israel prosecuted in the International Criminal Court in The Hague before receiving any benefit or recognition.

The refugee issue that led Palestinian leaders to reject past peace plans will no longer be regarded as a responsibility for Israel in any way. There would be no right of return for Arabs abroad, except to the Palestinian entity that could potentially be created in the unlikely scenario that all aforementioned conditions are met.

Like in any plan that is American and not Israeli, there are drawbacks for the Jewish state. The majority of the land in Judea and Samaria could theoretically not end up part of Israel.

This would give the Arabs living in those areas a contiguous area of land in which to live and vote. However, the international community will no longer be able to accuse Israel of occupying Palestinian land or compare the Jewish state to regimes maligned in recent history.

If the conditions are met, the Palestinians may receive what is called a state. But it would not be a state as a nation-state has been perceived before. All security would remain with Israel.

Only in the unlikely scenario of every condition being met by the Palestinians, there could be land that was promised to the Jewish people by God in the Torah that we would not keep, and that is of course very painful. It is understandable why some leaders of Jewish communities in Judea and Samaria decided to reject the plan for those reasons at first. Clearly, further analysis is required in regard to this Torah issue.

However, there is no gainsaying that the world has come a very long way, and the differences between this and all previous plans are inescapable.

The political circumstances of the timing of the plan's release are also undeniable but must not get in the way of implementing it immediately. The Knesset needs to act now and not wait for elections.

Blue and White leader Benny Gantz endorsed the plan. He should not push to wait for its implementation until Israel finally has a long-awaited government.

Prime Minister Benjamin Netanyahu brought about this plan after withstanding unprecedented pressure from Trump's predecessor, Barack Obama, and many other detractors. He understands that there is a narrow opportunity to act now as the American election approaches and other world issues overtake the news cycle.

In the final analysis, there is no reason to wait when the best deal ever imaginable is there on the table, ready for immediate implementation.

To wait would be an insult to President Trump, Jared Kushner, Ivanka Trump, Ambassador David Friedman, envoys Jason Greenblatt, Avi Berkowitz and Brian Hook and the rest of President Trump's spectacular staff who worked so hard on this plan.

Israel must show immediate gratitude to them for a plan that is beyond brilliant and undeniably trumps all others.

The Algemeiner

Trump's peace plan breaks new ground

The time has come for American Jewish groups to wake up and smell the positivity.

FEBRUARY 3, 2020

In this week's Torah portion, Moses displayed great courage by standing up to Pharaoh, the leader of the world's greatest nation at the time, who insisted on not letting the Jewish people go despite Egypt suffering plague after plague. But Moses never got the reward he so desired: entering the promised land.

Israeli Prime Minister Benjamin Netanyahu has arguably fared much better.

In May 2011, Netanyahu stood up to the leader of the world's greatest empire at the time, Barack Obama, as he attempted to impose a harsh diplomatic plan upon Israel based on its pre-1967 borders. Obama unveiled the plan while Netanyahu was en route to Washington, in the ultimate ambush.

Netanyahu's reward came on Jan. 28, when Obama's successor, U.S. President Donald Trump, unveiled a peace plan that Netanyahu called "the opportunity of the century."

American Jewish leaders should recognize what a gift President Trump has given Israel and the Jewish people, and express appropriate gratitude.

Instead of unveiling a fait accompli on the eve of a visit by the Israeli prime minister, without listening to him first, the president first listened not only to Netanyahu but also to the leader of his main political rival, Blue and White leader Benny Gantz.

And instead of a plan calling for Israel to withdraw from nearly all of what are called settlements, under Trump's plan Israel will be able to keep almost all of them and annex sizable portions of Judea and Samaria, the biblical heartland of the Jewish people.

Instead of a plan that calls for Israel to withdraw from land first in hopes that the Palestinians will concede on the refugee issue afterward, this plan calls for Israel to apply Israeli law to its land first and only gives the Palestinians a state later on, if they accept conditions that they are very unlikely to accept, like demilitarizing Gaza.

Instead of sending a message to the world that America is unhappy with Israel and inviting other countries to pressure the Jewish state, President Trump has sent a message to the world that the path to Washington goes through Jerusalem.

That message has been heard loud and clear across the globe. Israel's President Reuven Rivlin said he initially expected four or five leaders to come to Jerusalem to mark the 75th anniversary of the liberation of Auschwitz. The fact that 45 ended up coming is a testament to the positive atmosphere emanating from the White House.

The best evidence of that is that the British royal family had boycotted Israel for seven decades, but there was Prince Charles, the heir to the throne, coming to Jerusalem just ahead of Brexit, which will leave the United Kingdom needing the United States more than ever.

In Trump's plan, Israel will retain control over its capital: an undivided Jerusalem. Not only Obama but also Bill Clinton and even George W. Bush tried to get Israel to relinquish parts of the historic Old City. A plan worked out while Bush was president even called for internationalizing the Old City under the leadership of five countries, including a new Palestinian state, Jordan and Saudi Arabia.

Trump's plan is, of course, not perfect. It would create an inevitably dangerous Palestinian state and require Israel to give up more territory, territory that God gave to Abraham for the Jewish people. Even if these stages never arrive due to the intransigence of Palestinian leaders, merely accepting these terms is a very painful concession on Israel's part.

But this plan is so much better than all of its predecessors that Israel and American Jewish groups must show proper appreciation. Both Netanyahu and Gantz did that before, during and after their meetings with Trump, reflecting the views of the consensus of the people of Israel.

Why have American Jewish groups not done the same? Even those that avoid U.S. and Israeli politics must realize how far Israel has come over the past decade.

The time has come for American Jewish groups to wake up and smell the positivity, and to thank Trump.

As the Hebrew saying goes, we have overcome Pharaoh, so we can overcome this. Even the complacency and indifference of too many American Jews in the face of the reward received from the most pro-Israel U.S. president ever can and must be overcome.

The Jerusalem Post

US Jews must urge Israelis to safeguard the Trump-Netanyahu relationship

Israel needs the best leader possible at this critical moment, and no one has more experience than Prime Minister Benjamin Netanyahu.

FEBRUARY 18, 2020

There are two adages that have been sacrosanct for decades when it comes to decisions about Israel's future.

One is that such decisions must be made by Israel's democratically elected government alone, and that American Jews who do not live in the Jewish state must keep their opinions about internal Israeli politics to themselves.

The other is that the Palestinians never miss an opportunity to miss an opportunity.

It may be controversial to say this, but at this fateful juncture for Israel's future, both of those adages that have withstood the test of time do not currently apply.

As someone who has advocated for Israel for decades and prayed for the Jewish state three times a day since its establishment, I cannot be silent, and neither should other Jewish leaders who understand the importance of the present moment in history.

I was privileged to be present in the White House when US President Donald Trump unveiled his Middle East peace plan, which is appropriately called both "Peace to Prosperity" and "The Deal of the Century." Hearing the details of the plan first-hand, I was extremely impressed by the hard work and in-depth research that went into it.

This plan would safeguard Israel's future and ensure its existence amid the security threats to the Jewish state that will never end. Maintaining

Israeli security – which was a challenge in previous plans proposed by previous American administrations – would no longer be an issue, because the IDF would maintain security control and protect both Israel and the entrances to where the Palestinians would continue to live.

As soon as the plan's maps are ready, the plan allows Israel to immediately start applying Israeli law to the lands where the Jews of Judea and Samaria live now and where our forefathers and mothers lived before.

There are Palestinian and European leaders and Democratic Party presidential candidates in the US who have criticized the plan, as was expected. It is not their opposition that could prevent the plan from getting carried out.

Amazingly, the plan is in danger of being held up and perhaps never even being implemented at all not because of any of them, but because of the voters in Israel's upcoming fateful election on March 2.

Israelis must be told that this plan must be implemented immediately to ensure Israel's long-term future, and it needs an experienced leader who has built a fruitful relationship with Trump. This is not the time for a dangerous change in Israeli leadership.

Israel needs the best leader possible at this critical moment, and no one has more experience than Prime Minister Benjamin Netanyahu. After President Trump's peace deal is implemented, there will be less need to have a monumental prime minister like him in place, and it will then be safer to take risks of electing a new leader.

This is not the time to initiate unnecessary negotiations with the Palestinians or wait for the support of the international community that would never come. This is the time to draw the maps of Israel's borders and start implementing the plan the moment the maps are ready, regardless of Israeli politics.

Waiting for a government to be formed in Israel to implement the plan would be a huge mistake, because there could be a fourth or even a fifth

Israeli election. President Trump waited patiently during the first two Israeli elections, but there is no guarantee that he will win a second term in office, so there is no time to waste.

The Netanyahu-Trump era must be maximized to the fullest, because we don't know who the next prime minister will be, who the next US president will be, or what will be the makeup of the next Congress. Listening to how uneducated some of the Democratic presidential candidates are on Israel reinforces the urgency of the moment at hand.

Religious Zionists in America have a particular responsibility to ensure that the plan gets implemented, because it would not have happened without us.

Religious Zionists have thankfully overcome – or at least balanced out – the left wing who can return to positions of influence in the future, both in the US and in Israel when Netanyahu is no longer in power. While religious Zionists will always be the backbone among Israel's supporters in the US, it is questionable whether self-proclaimed progressive American Jews and their children can be counted on to support Israel two decades from now.

The plan is currently bilateral between the US and Israel, though American leaders have said they hope that the Palestinians will join it in the future. That gives Americans and Israelis equal footing in ensuring that it gets shepherded toward implementation as soon as possible.

Not only can American Jewish leaders speak, we have an obligation to make our voices heard by Israelis as they go to vote. We must tell Israelis that waiting too long could result in Israel missing the ultimate opportunity – the opportunity of the century.

Missing this opportunity would be a tragedy that would be added to the long list of too many tragedies the Jewish people have endured throughout our history.

Israel National News

Interview

FEBRUARY 20, 2020

Martin Oliner, Co-President of the Religious Zionists of America, Chairman of the Center for Righteousness and Integrity, a committee member of the Jewish Agency, spoke to Arutz Sheva about the "deal of the century" and what he believes is necessary in order for it to work.

"The president was clear, he ' have been clearer, that we have the plan of a century, the deal of the century," Oliner said, adding that "all that was required to be done, to move it forward, unlike any paradigm in the past, is for the people of Israel to adopt and move forward with it."

"What's critical is for them to go forward with annexation, move it along, and there's no objection. There's a four-year period for which Palestinians can come to the table, if they meet certain conditions - conditions that are obvious, conditions of peace, and it brings to us the peace that we need in our time, immediately."

Oliner emphasized: "The only thing that needs to be done again is for the community of Israel, the politicians of Israel, to move forward immediately, to bring about a government led in part, if not in full, by the current Prime Minister [Binyamin Netanyahu], who has this extraordinary relationship with the President of the United States. The times have changed, the world has changed, what needs to be done is for everyone to rally around this Prime Minister to ensure the adaptation of the deal of the century."

When asked about the reports that Israel had been asked to wait until after March 2020's elections to apply annexation, and that mapping needed to be done first, Oliner responded: "That wasn't what we said."

"What was said originally, and at all times was that mapping was necessary. There are obvious parts of this that need to be done BUT that should not prevent the moving forward immediately."

He asked: "The Arab community seems to be the one that never misses an opportunity to miss an opportunity. Are we going to be in their footsteps, are we going to follow our friends, our cousins, and not move forward immediately? The clear answer from us has to be, 'Yes, this is what we're agreeing to, we agree completely, let's get it going.'"

Regarding the fact that the Netanyahu government has not yet put forward a bill on annexing the areas in question, Oliner said: "Every possible obstacle has been placed in front of our Prime Minister, Prime Minister of the State of Israel, and he has responded with courage and fortitude. That courage and fortitude needs to be continued."

"This is the one time where it's critical, important beyond any measure, for all Israelis to rally around this Prime Minister because he's the one for the moment who has the relationship and can pull this off. The deal of the century is dependent upon people, people and [the] only people today have the fortitude, the ability, the brightness to move it forward is the blessed Prime Minister that we have today."

The Jerusalem Post

Time for Israel, US to overcome COVID-19 and POLITICS-2020

MARCH 26, 2020

I have been an admirer of the Jewish state since before it existed, and a constant admirer of US President Donald Trump since long before he became president. My thoughts on both have appeared regularly on these pages.

As Israel made the desert bloom and became the Start-Up Nation, I only became more in awe of its accomplishments, in the worst neighborhood, against all odds.

As President Trump revealed his policies on the Middle East, I became increasingly infatuated with his wisdom.

But over the past month, since the first Israeli tested positive for the coronavirus, I have been shaking my head at what has been happening in Israel, and deeply concerned that the US is always a step behind the virus.

Prime Minister Benjamin Netanyahu is absolutely right when he says he has led Israel in crucial, stringent measures against the virus; steps that have been ahead of the curve around the world. President Trump is similarly correct when he notes that his travel ban on China saved countless lives.

Austrian Chancellor Sebastian Kurz even said he "thanked God" for a conversation he had with Netanyahu, in which Netanyahu told him to "wake up and do something." The 33-year-old Kurz, who sees the 70-year-old Netanyahu as a mentor, has used Israel as a model in taking serious action to counter the spread of the virus.

Likewise, many world leaders and vocal Democrats have praised the Trump-Pence task force that is contending with the coronavirus in America for its creativity and for the action it mandated.

So why in Israel have the leaders of Blue and White and other opposition parties like Labor and Yisrael Beytenu not rushed to join Netanyahu's government and to help him guide Israel through these troubled times?

Is there no humility in Blue and White leader Benny Gantz? As a former general, does he not realize the benefits of being steered by an experienced, decisive leader?

Clearly this is a war. Israel must treat it as such.

If there was an attack on Israel by Iran, God forbid, wouldn't Israelis come together? Don't they realize that in some ways, this is worse?

At the time this is being written, five Israelis have died from the virus. The first death, Aryeh Even, was even more a tragedy, because he was a survivor of the Holocaust.

More than 1,000 Israelis have contracted the virus in just a month. Israel's record low unemployment rate has skyrocketed overnight. Many tens of thousands are in quarantine and too many people are suffering.

The situation in the US is staggering. At the time I'm writing this, more than 55,000 have tested positive for the virus and nearly have died from it. Those numbers will be much higher by the time this is published.

Nevertheless, Israelis keep bickering about petty politics. They are trying to pass frivolous laws that are anti-Bibi, or pro-Bibi, instead of just making sure elderly Israelis will continue to be able to breathe! Unlike the US, the effort to "impeach" Netanyahu
never stops.

In this regard, Israel has even fallen behind the United States, where hyperpolarization has in many cases been suspended for a higher good. In my state of New York, our Democrat Gov. Andrew Cuomo is working elbow-to-elbow with Republican President Donald Trump for the greater good.

Although President Trump has acted under the Defense Production Act, he has refused to maximize its potential. It needs to be used in at least three ways.

First, we need a Manhattan Project similar to the one that created the atomic bomb in World War II. In order to win this war, vaccines, treatments and tests are required.

The American administration should nationalize the effort by ordering all research labs and scientists in government, academia and private industry to join together. The government should pay for this effort.

Lockdown and related rules must be uniformly enforced throughout the country.

Second, the president should nationalize and lead an effort to ensure that all needed hospital beds and equipment, such as ventilators, masks and gowns are available to peak virus levels. In addition, the government should guarantee that all essentials, from sanitizers to toilet paper, are fully available.

Finally, the president should continue to care for those who have been put out of work by providing wage and price guidelines that will guarantee all hard-working people an unemployment wage and that will counter price-gouging.

Similar measures should be happening in Israel as well. But like everything else in both countries, it depends on politics.

At least we in America know who the president of the United States will be until January. Israel could have two more elections by then!

This is the time for Gantz to join a 60-day emergency government under Netanyahu. If that does not end up being enough, he could sign up for another 60 days.

This is the time for President Trump to take complete charge, regardless of the political ramifications.

Disregarding petty politics would allow the US and Israel to continue leading the world, and most importantly, to spread hope instead of fear at this time of a proliferating pandemic.

The Jerusalem Post

Give Netanyahu his lasting legacy with annexation

Israel needs to apply sovereignty to its land, and it may very well need to do this sooner rather than later. This can give Netanyahu a lasting legacy.

MAY 13, 2020

As Israel begins to emerge from the coronavirus relatively unscathed compared to other countries of its size, nightmare predictions have not come true, thanks to the leadership of Prime Minister Benjamin Netanyahu and the impressive discipline and resilience of Israelis.

Now imagine that instead of Netanyahu leading the way, and his people implementing his decisions, a superpower tried to impose its will on the Jewish state and dictate key policies that would have a major impact on all its citizens.

Perhaps people with short memories cannot recall, but that used to happen all the time before Israel's best-ever friend in the White House, Donald Trump, became president of the United States. Both Democratic and Republican presidents regularly tried to pressure Israel to make concessions that a consensus of Israelis opposed.

Unsurprisingly, Israelis do not want to return to the bad old days.

But the Middle East advisers who worked for presidents Bill Clinton and Barack Obama apparently do. Despite their unquestionable experience, they fail to appreciate the changing times and the shift to a new Middle East paradigm, in which Israel is respected by most of its neighbors.

Those advisers, Dennis Ross and David Makovsky, penned an article for the Times of Israel titled, "On annexation, Netanyahu must choose a lasting legacy." In the article, they warned against Israel's intentions to implement President Trump's Middle East peace plan, especially the clauses related to applying Israeli sovereignty to parts of Judea and Samaria, the biblical heartland of the Jewish people.

"History will not take a kind view to annexation of all settlements, a step that in any case Netanyahu himself did not intend less than a decade ago," they wrote. "We hope the premier draws a lesson from his key predecessors and chooses a worthy legacy, one that ensures Israel's Jewish and democratic character is secure for generations."

Makovsky and Ross gleaned those "intentions" of the prime minister less than a decade ago from a speech given by Netanyahu to the Knesset on May 16, 2011. They suggest that Bibi stated he would seek to annex only a fraction of settlements as part of a negotiated deal with the Palestinians based on the consensus of the Israeli public.

"We agree that we must maintain the settlement blocs," they pointed out that he said in the speech. "There is widespread agreement that the settlement blocs must remain within the State of Israel."

Makovsky and Ross cited this quote that they took out of context as evidence that Netanyahu wanted to evacuate all Jewish communities over the pre-1967 border except what are defined as settlement blocs.

Nothing can be further from the truth.

In that speech, Netanyahu defined what at the time was the Israeli consensus. In what was a profound statement back then, Netanyahu was pointing out that even the Left in Israel favored keeping the settlement blocs.

The proper way to interpret what Netanyahu said was that while settlements not in blocs were supported by the Right that he led, the blocs were supported by the Israeli Right, center and Left.

In their sanctimonious assessment of Netanyahu, they say he was correct in articulating the Israeli consensus, but they neglect to mention that the consensus in Israel has changed significantly since then.

Shortly after that speech, UNESCO voted to recognize Palestine as a state, a decision that made Netanyahu more vigilant. Since then, there have been rockets, mortars, terrorist tunnels, shootings, stabbings and incendiary kites, all of which persuaded Israelis to take a harder line with the Palestinians.

The Israeli consensus now mirrors the positions in Trump's peace plan, including the clauses enabling Israel to apply sovereignty to parts of Judea and Samaria.

An Israel Democracy Institute poll taken last month asked Israelis if they would support "a plan coordinated with the United States for applying sovereignty to parts of the West Bank/Judea and Samaria if it would be brought for the government and the Knesset's approval."

More than half the respondents, 51.7%, answered affirmatively. Only 27.9% said they would oppose such a move.

Since that is the consensus now, Ross and Makovsky should be pushing Netanyahu and other Israelis to implement the plan, not to reject it. They should be telling the 450,000 Jews of Judea and Samaria that they will never have to move.

At the very least, they should be silently repenting for all their failures in past peace processes in which they tried to push Israel to make concessions and evacuate settlements.

So why is an article on Israel's second-most read English news site, written by two former Democratic White House advisers, worthy of attention?

Simply put, an American election is coming up, and it is possible that Trump could be defeated by former vice president Joe Biden. If that happens, Ross and Makovsky could once again have the ear of an American president, something that could be very dangerous for the future of Israel.

Makovsky and Ross would take the US-Israel relationship back to the bad old days of the US pressuring Israel. They would take the Middle East backward to when mediators shuttled between Ramallah and Jerusalem, and frequently sided with Ramallah against America's best friend in the region. Israel's progress with its neighbors would be set back.

Former Clinton and Obama staffers are already advising Biden about how to handle Israel, and misleading him, and it is already starting to show.

In a statement to the Jewish Telegraphic Agency on Tuesday, Biden said the US should press Israel not to take any actions that jeopardize a two-state solution.

"A priority now for the cause of Israeli-Palestinian peace should be resuming our dialogue with the Palestinians, and pressing Israel not to take actions that make a two-state solution impossible," Biden said.

Israel does not need pressing. It needs to apply sovereignty to its land, and it may very well need to do this sooner rather than later.

This can indeed give Netanyahu a lasting legacy, and it would also preempt future nightmares for the Jewish state.

The Jerusalem Post

UAE and Israel: A match made in heaven

This agreement is a match made in heaven, wedding the technology of Israel with the economic powerhouse of the UAE.

AUGUST 14, 2020

Earlier this month, the Jewish people celebrate the joyous holiday of Tu Be'Av, the date on the Jewish calendar that focuses on love and commitment.

Little did we know, but at the time, US President Donald Trump, Israeli Prime Minister Benjamin Netanyahu and United Arab Emirates Crown Prince Mohammed bin Zayed Al Nahyan were putting the finishing touches on an agreement formalizing the bond between Israel and the UAE.

This agreement is a match made in heaven, wedding the technology of Israel with the economic powerhouse of the UAE.

Only those who have spent time in both countries, as I have, can appreciate how magnificent an opportunity this agreement is, not only for Israel and the UAE but also for making the entire world a better place. Both countries are at the forefront of success in a changing global world.

Dubai has a skyline that rivals Manhattan and has become a very important financial center. It is a place of tolerance, not just relative to the rest of the Arab world. Its population is vibrant and diverse. It has become a home to American universities and a hub for key airlines.

Israel's innovation has impressed the world and become a model, especially for other small countries. Its accomplishments have come despite having few natural resources and a turbulent political system.

After peace agreements with Egypt and then Jordan failed to result in increased ties between Israel and other Arab countries, this deal opens up the Arab and Muslim world to Israel through Dubai and enables mutually beneficial commerce and trade. The Crown Prince deserves much praise for his courage in making the deal.

This agreement creates opportunities for cooperation in agriculture and tourism as well as technology that is needed more than ever during the international health and economic crises caused by the COVID-19 pandemic. It would be very symbolic if the lifting of the animosity between these two countries will lead to the breakthrough the world has been waiting for and praying for.

As expected with any accomplishment of President Trump and Prime Minister Netanyahu, critics on both the Left and Right have been quick to downplay and dismiss this historic agreement.

Palestinian Authority chairman Mahmoud Abbas said he viewed the deal as an affront to the Palestinian people. Abbas's criticism is proof of the agreement's necessity and its potential success.

None of the concessions Israel made for decades led to the Palestinians reciprocating. Rather than make the concessions necessary to help their own people, Abbas and other Palestinian leaders stalled for time, resorted to violence and incitement and missed countless opportunities.

This agreement should be a wake-up call to the Palestinians that no one is waiting for them to overcome their stubbornness anymore. Whether they like it or not, those days are now officially over. Their ability to hold Israel hostage has been lost forever.

Perhaps seeing a leading Arab country pursue the agreement with Israel that they should have made decades ago will finally be what brings the Palestinians back to the negotiating table.

But whenever they do come back, they will find that while they were stalling, the paradigm changed. This agreement with UAE is the first of what will become the new trend: Instead of land for peace, from now on, Israel will be trading peace for peace.

Israel will no longer relinquish land and evacuate Jews from their homes in return for calm and instead receive rockets, terror tunnels and suicide bombers in return. The Palestinians will have to overcome their internal divides, their corruption and their misplaced priorities, or they will be rightly forgotten.

With all due respect to the Palestinians, the UAE is much more important for Israel's future. The Gross Domestic Product of the UAE is 414.2 billion dollars, more than 28 times the GDP of the Palestinian Authority. Its ability to affect thePalestinian Authority cannot be overstated.

This agreement can lead to peace deals with other Muslim countries I have visited, including Bahrain and Qatar and eventually Saudi Arabia. We pray for peace three times a day, and thanks to President Trump, our prayers are bearing fruit.

This was the goal of President Trump's peace plan from day one, and skeptics who doubted that he could bring about peace in the Middle East are invited to eat their hat. Ambassador David Friedman, Trump advisers Jared Kushner and Avi Berkowitz, and Friedman's chief of staff Aryeh Lightstone all deserve praise for their extraordinary accomplishment.

Despite incorrect reports to the contrary, they will continue to work toward applying sovereignty in Judea and Samaria, which has now become easier, not harder, now that the proper environment for implementation has been created. Israeli politicians to the Right of Netanyahu are absolutely wrong to downplay the achievements for Israel in this agreement due to their concerns about sovereignty's suspension. As a practical matter, that suspension does not affect the situation on the ground and gives credence by its very terms to a later declaration of sovereignty rather than annexation.

But while applying sovereignty would realistically require President Trump's re-election in November, this agreement between Israel and the UAE will remain for posterity, no matter who will live in the White House after the inauguration in January.

This deal will be added to the long list of decisions made by President Trump that will leave him remembered as America's best president ever for Israel. The list includes recognizing Jerusalem as Israel's capital, moving the US embassy to Jerusalem, declaring the legality of the Jewish communities in Judea and Samaria, recognizing Israeli sovereignty over the Golan Heights, breaking the awful deal with Iran and supporting Israel completely at the United Nations.

For the past three and a half years, the road to Washington has passed through Jerusalem, and the Arab world knows that, which has made the entire world safer. The UAE deal with the Crown Prince is a crowning achievement for President Trump in his first term and makes him worthy of receiving another four years to accomplish even more.

Some American Jews may not love President Trump, but this is the time to express gratitude to him for everything he has done for Israel. If that happens, the day that this deal was announced should go down in history as a day to be celebrated.

The Jerusalem Post

Why Americans in Israel must vote for Trump

Despite Israel's crisis being solved, some 300,000 Israelis can still exercise their democratic right to cast ballots in an election in November.

SEPTEMBER 4, 2020

Were it not for the agreement reached between Prime Minister Benjamin Netanyahu's Likud and Alternate Prime Minister Benny Gantz's Blue and White party on Monday night, Israelis would have gone to the polls in November.

Despite Israel's crisis being solved, some 300,000 Israelis can still exercise their democratic right to cast ballots in an election in November.

That is roughly the number of residents of Israel who are eligible to vote by absentee ballot in the November 3 election in the United States.

Four years ago, there was a high-profile campaign in Israel for then-Republican presidential candidate Donald Trump. Stickers bearing Trump's name in Hebrew were handed out in Israeli malls, and the president addressed a campaign rally in Jerusalem's Old City by video.

This time, Americans in Israel have been relatively silent about the US election, when they really should be shouting out loud and going to vote in droves.

On the one hand, it is understandable why there was so much more enthusiasm and motivation about voting four years ago. Americans who care about Israel had just endured eight years of Barack Obama and Joe Biden in power and saw the way they advanced a deal with Iran while throwing Israel under the bus at the United Nations.

They had every right to be terrified that Obama's secretary of state, Hillary Clinton, would continue his policies that endangered Israel's future existence and the special relationship between Israel and the United States.

But on the other hand, four years ago, American voters in Israel could only guess what they would be getting if Trump became president. They heard his campaign promises to move America's embassy to Jerusalem and defend Israel at the UN, but who believes what any politician says during a campaign?

Now, after four wonderful years of making both America and Israel great again, President Trump's actions speak even louder than his words, which is saying a lot.

The move of America's embassy to Jerusalem is no longer a promise made by president after president but an actual building with an American flag flying high with pride in Israel's capital that is finally recognized by the United States. The building has the names of President Donald Trump and Vice President Mike Pence and always will.

A few minutes' drive away from the embassy are thriving Jewish communities in Judea and Samaria that the US government no longer calls illegal settlements and no longer instigates an international uproar when a family builds a home for their grown children across the street.

This American administration recognized Israel's control over the Golan Heights after the previous administration of Obama and Biden would not even recognize that the Syrian regime had to be punished for using chemical weapons against its own people.

The Obama-Biden government made a despicable deal with Iran that ended soon after Donald Trump became president of the United States. Relentless American pressure continues on Iran, but it would obviously end immediately if Biden becomes president and seeks another deal with Iran at Israel's expense.
Even the UN, where the Obama-Biden administration gave Israel a parting pie in the face before they left office, became a much less hostile place for the Jewish State as soon as President Trump took over. Biden did nothing to stop Obama from pushing forward UN Security Council Resolution 2334, which called Jews living in their Biblical heartland a "flagrant violation" of international law with "no legal validity."

While Obama and Biden chose to battle against Israel in the final months of their term, President Trump is ending this term by facilitating Israel making peace with its Arab Muslim neighbors. The deal with the UAE is already fostering economic cooperation that will benefit the entire world and could even help put a stop to COVID-19.

So if they voted four years ago, how could Americans in Israel neglect to perform their civic duty this time around? How can they not have hakarat hatov – gratefulness – to President Trump for all the good he has done for the two countries they love?

Even Israelis from firmly red and blue states have to cast ballots. Their votes may not end up making a difference in the electoral college, but they will be counted by the Trump campaign as the ultimate thank you note.

Their ballots could also end up helping key local races and perhaps will be the deciding votes that enable the Republican Party to maintain control of the Senate. If Americans in Israel voted four years ago before they had heard of Ilhan Omar or Rashida Tlaib or knew what AOC stood for, how could they not vote now, when the progressive wing has become such a dominant force in the Democratic Party?

For centuries, Jews were deprived of the right to vote by despicable anti-Israel leaders in countries around the world. Now it is easier than ever to vote for the most pro-Israel leader of the free world in the history of mankind.

This article is intended to serve as a wake-up call to Americans in Israel. They were spared the burden of voting in yet another intense Israeli election, but they have the responsibility to cast their ballots in another election that will go a long way to deciding Israel's future.

The Jerusalem Post

Voting for Trump as a multi-issue voter

Americans should not only be voting for Trump because of what he has done for Israel but rather what he has done for America.

OCTOBER 26, 2020

There are many American Jews who will be voting for US President Donald Trump because of his support for Israel.

These so-called one-issue voters will use their ballots to express gratitude to the president for recognizing Jerusalem as Israel's capital, moving the US Embassy there, recognizing Israel's sovereignty over the Golan Heights, the peace agreements with UAE and Bahrain and breaking America's dangerous deal with Iran.

But there are many more reasons to vote for Trump. Americans should not only be voting for Trump because of what he has done for Israel. They should be voting for Trump because of what he has done for America.

Let's start with the economy. Under Trump, the gross domestic product grew by 4.1% in 2019 and by 5.4% in 2018, numbers that were previously thought impossible to reach.

The Trump administration's tax cuts save thousands of dollars a year for American families. Trump's Tax Cuts and Jobs Act, which he signed into law on December 22, 2017, was the largest overhaul of the tax code in three decades.

Trump created 6.6 million jobs in his first three years in office, a 4.4% increase over the 152.2 million people working at the end of Obama's term. A large portion of the jobs came from companies returning to the US from China and other countries, due to incentives Trump initiated.

He also created thousands of jobs thanks to his energy policies rescinding fracking restrictions in December 2017. The president signed an executive order in April 2019 that made it easier to build oil and gas pipelines, which made America the world's largest petroleum producer.

Like in every country, the economic numbers will not be as good in 2020, due to the challenges of fighting COVID-19. But Americans need to be thankful that Trump was running the economy during the coronavirus crisis, because he minimized its damage to both our livelihood and our lives.

The 225,000 Americans who lost their lives due to COVID-19 are each a terrible tragedy. But it had been estimated that 2.2 million Americans could have died from the virus, and that did not happen, thanks to the policies of Trump.

From closing down the country to anyone coming from China, to encouraging the development of rapid testing, Trump has done what is necessary to minimize the harm done by the coronavirus.

All predictions that hospitals would be overwhelmed were proven false. Trump made sure that there would be enough ventilators for anyone who needed them. He used executive orders when necessary to procure ventilators, masks and other protective gear.

Now his goal is to ensure that a vaccine will be available to all Americans as soon as possible. Operation Warp Speed is a public and private partnership initiated by the Trump administration to facilitate and accelerate the development, manufacturing and distribution of vaccines, therapeutics and diagnostics.

There have been incentives provided to companies to develop a vaccine, and the company that succeeds in completing a ready-to-use vaccine first will be rewarded. Meanwhile, the development of therapeutic medicine has saved lives.

There is no doubt that Trump could have set a better example and should have done more to encourage the wearing of masks. Sure, his demeanor and personality could be off-putting to some. But his policies have been spot-on – successful, powerful, productive and patriotic.

Trump also protected Americans through his support of law enforcement. He put a stop to the chaos, violent riots and looting that had shut down major cities.

The rioters took over federal buildings and tried to burn them down. Trump restored order and stability. His continued support for law enforcement will help ensure the security of Americans in the future.

The United States returned to the forefront of the international fight against terrorism under Trump. The world is a safer place without arch-terrorists Abu Bakr al-Baghdadi and Qasem Soleimani.

The media's predictions of mass violence following targeted killings were incorrect in retrospect. The unprofessional treatment of Trump by the media over the past four years is another reason to defiantly vote to reelect the president.

Social media accounts have been suspended and shut down for political reasons. Rights and privileges have been taken away by those who have shown no tolerance for opposing views.

America cannot and should not be manipulated by big tech and some of the fourth estate. Free speech is our inviolable right.

Defeating the Left and stopping its abuse of power is yet another reason to cast a ballot for the president. Warnings of undemocratic steps like packing the Supreme Court or adding two states for partisan reasons demonstrates the Left's manipulation of the integrity of our revered Constitution.

Leftist radicals have been destroying monuments. But they cannot change history. History has proven that America is the ultimate safe haven for people regardless of their views, race, religion and ethnicity. All Americans should be thankful to live in our great country.

In the first term of Donald Trump as president, he made America great again, and he also made the US-Israel relationship greater than ever.

Trump's second term can be greater on all these fronts. But it depends on him receiving enough votes, whether they come from one-issue voters or those who care about a variety of issues when they cast their ballots.

The Jerusalem Post

WZO victory achieved through 'wall-to-wall' coalition

The signing ceremony brought together a cross section of the Jewish people, continuing the tradition of the WZO going back to the days of Theodore Herzl.

OCTOBER 27, 2020

After two weeks of headlines about a "hostile takeover of the World Zionist Organization" by the Right and the Orthodox, representatives of political parties, Jewish organizations and religious streams across the religious and political spectrum came together in Jerusalem last Thursday to sign a wall-to-wall coalition agreement.

The signing ceremony brought together a cross section of the Jewish people, continuing the tradition of the WZO going back to the days of Theodore Herzl.

Mizrachi's representative at the ceremony was Avraham Duvdevani, who has been following in Herzl's footsteps. He will leave his post as WZO chairman to become head of Keren Kayemet, both posts once held by the visionary Zionist leader.

Even Herzl could not have dreamed that one day his successor would be a religious Zionist who wears a crocheted kippa. The truth is that even a decade ago, it would have been unimaginable that Mizrachi would take over such venerable institutions.

This history happened not because of any back room deals in Jerusalem but because proud religious Zionists in the United States demonstrated their commitment to Israel's future by casting ballots for the Orthodox Israel Coalition in the American Zionist Movement's voting online from January to March.

The coalition united the Orthodox Union, Yeshiva University, Touro College, Bnei Akiva, AMIT, the RCA, the National Council of Young Israel and Torah Mitzion. There were also religious Zionist delegates to the Zionist Congress from Australia, Europe, Russia, South America, South Africa and Israel.

Rick Jacobs, the president of the Union for Reform Judaism, warned on Twitter of "an extreme right wing attempt to dominate" the WZO. But the agreement signed fairly distributes control over Zionist institutions and departments to a wide range of Jewish organizations and factions, from Orthodox to Reform and from Right to Left.

The Mizrachi faction that will lead Keren Kayemet includes representatives of the Yamina party on the Right, as well as the Derech Eretz party that ran with Blue and White in the last three elections for Knesset. Since its founding in 1902 by Rabbi Yitzchak Yaacov Reines at a world conference of religious Zionists in Vilnius, the Mizrachi has been home to religious Zionists with a host of different political views.

Religious Zionists have helped settle the Land of Israel, building beautiful communities and have even been among the leaders of Peace Now advocating territorial concessions. They have been generals and pacifists. They are the leaders of yeshivot and universities, Torah scholars and hi-tech executives.

After it heads the KKL for two years, Mizrachi will have control for three years over the WZO's Settlement Division, which like KKL, works to develop Israel's periphery in the Negev and Galilee, a goal that is the key to the future of a country that is overly populated in its center and underpopulated in its periphery.

Mizrachi will also head the WZO's Education Department, reflecting a commitment to education that has been the focus of religious Zionists for centuries. Religious Zionist parties have made a point of asking for the Education Ministry in almost all Israeli governments.

When there was concern that funding would be stopped for Masa, Mizrachi stepped in to solve the problem and help students from across the spectrum come to Israel on long-term programs. Upgrading stipends for Masa was a central campaign promise of the Orthodox Israel Coalition that we intend to keep.

Unlike sectarian factions that serve themselves when given power, Mizrachi aims to serve all of Klal Israel - all its sectors, streams and sub-groups. The central tenets of religious Zionism are advancing the Torah of Israel, the Land of Israel and the entire nation of Israel, not just ourselves.

That is why our victory in the Zionist Movement election is really a win for Jews around the world who care about the future of the Jewish state.

Due to the coronavirus, the Zionist Congress was held virtually. But its positive impact on the future of Israel and the Jewish Diaspora will be unmistakably real.

Mizrachi - the Religious Zionists of America, will use their greater influence to benefit the State of Israel and klal Israel - all branches, sectors and streams. We will continue to be the bridge builders, facilitating friendship and collegiality among Jews around the world. At such a divisive time for the Jewish people in the US, Israel and around the world, this has never been more important.

When asked where the emphasis is in religious-Zionism, my answer has always been in the hyphen that connects them. We are proud to be both observant keepers of commandments and lovers of the homeland of the Jewish people.

With gratitude to God, we will continue to spread His light and help Israel, the light unto the nations.

The Jerusalem Post

Take your time in dismissing Donald Trump

President deprived of pre-election Pfizer vaccine boost.

NOVEMBER 12, 2020

Prime Minister Benjamin Netanyahu has faced harsh criticism for his decision to not yet call Democratic candidate Joe Biden the "president-elect."

Israeli politicians - from opposition leader Yair Lapid to Alternate Prime Minister Benny Gantz - have accused Netanyahu of harming the bipartisan US-Israel relationship. Media outlets, including The Jerusalem Post, have criticized Netanyahu for being sensitive and careful in his congratulatory message to Biden.

But Netanyahu - who is correctly impatient in trying to get Pfizer's coronavirus vaccine for Israelis as US President Donald Trump did for Americans - was absolutely right to be patient when it comes to American politics. He was smart to be cautious in allowing the remaining vote counting and essential legal procedures to run their course.

The following tweet does not come from any right-wing Israeli or American politician. It was posted by former Democratic presidential candidate Hillary Clinton on Wednesday, November 4, the same day Netanyahu congratulated Biden without calling him the president-elect.

"We'll know the election results when every ballot is counted," she wrote. "That's how democracy works."

It took Hillary three more days to tweet that "the voters have spoken" and chose Biden, after she came under tremendous political pressure and looked like a sore loser from her own race.

By contrast, no harm has been done to Israel by Netanyahu being especially sensitive to the current political situation in the United States. If anything, he and Israel may end up being rewarded by President

Donald Trump, who will remain in the office for at least another two months, if not four more years.

Netanyahu has demonstrated that he is grateful to the president for everything he has done for Israel, including recognizing Jerusalem as Israel's capital, moving the embassy, breaking the dangerous Iran deal, recognizing Israel's sovereignty over the Golan Heights and bringing about normalization between Israel and the United Arab Emirates, Bahrain and Sudan.

There could be more peace deals on the way, or perhaps more steps to recognize the rights of Jews to live in communities in the Biblical heartland of the Jewish people in Judea and Samaria.

Israelis need to respect that despite the haste in the American press prematurely declaring Biden the winner, President Trump has earned his right to look into allegations of voting irregularities and weigh his legal options. The president's charges of fake news are legitimate.

President Trump has fought an uphill battle against all odds. The fact that more than 70 million people voted for him after four years of bad press is nothing short of a miracle and a tremendous vote of confidence in his leadership, his abilities and his domestic and foreign policies.

Regardless of what the final outcome will be, it is indisputable that the race was so close that even one critical news development could have made all the difference.

Imagine if Pfizer would have announced positive results for its coronavirus vaccine one week earlier, before the election and not after.

Pfizer's top management has admitted that the lab testing of their study participants was suspended before the election and the results of the study were in effect frozen.

William Gruber, Pfizer's senior vice president of vaccine clinical research and development, told STAT News that Pfizer and BioNTech had decided to stop having their lab confirm cases of Covid-19 in the study and left their samples in storage. If Pfizer had held to its original plan, the data would likely have been available in October, as its CEO, Albert Bourla, initially promised.

Bourla and other company leaders repeatedly suggested that they may have data in October. They could have said that any announcement would be guided by science, not politics, but they instead raised expectations.

Coincidentally, Bloomberg News Service has revealed that the Federal Drug Administration was involved in Pfizer's decisions to change their timetable for testing, which led to the successful results not being revealed before the election.

President Trump's success in bringing a vaccine before the election but not receiving credit for it was just one "coincidence" among many that were to the detriment of President Trump and could have made a major difference.

I can only wish that Democrats in America and the anti-Trump media could be as patient, careful and smart as Netanyahu.

Israelis should consider themselves lucky to have such leadership, as Israel approaches its own election.

The Jerusalem Post

Not enough done to stymie scourge of antisemitism

Jews from coast to coast have been targeted at synagogues, restaurants and on the streets.

MAY 26, 2021

MAY has been Jewish American Heritage Month, which is supposed to recognize and celebrate the achievements of American Jews and their contributions to the United States.

But this past month has instead seen a massive surge in antisemitic attacks, verbal abuse and hate crimes, terrifying Jews across the US.

Jews from coast to coast have been targeted at synagogues, restaurants and on the streets.
Jews praying at a Borough Park synagogue last Shabbat were afraid to leave, because thugs outside yelled "kill the Jews" and "free Palestine."

The Los Angeles Police Department is probing a hate crime in which Jews were attacked outside a sushi restaurant.

In Bal Harbour, Florida, a Jew vacationing with his family was harassed by men in a car who shouted "die Jew" and threatened to rape his wife and daughter. A "Walk for Israel" rally near Chicago was disrupted by violent protesters.

The Anti-Defamation League has reported 26 instances of antisemitism since May 10, but most incidents go unreported.

The surge has, of course, been connected to Israel's anti-Hamas Operation Guardian of the Walls against terror from the Gaza Strip. Other wars and military operations in the Middle East have led in the past to an upswing in hate against Jews in America.

Former senator Daniel Patrick Moynihan, who famously defended Israel from the UN declaring Zionism is racism 25 years ago, also said anti-Zionism is antisemitism.

But nowadays antisemites in America no longer need any excuses. Their hate has been legitimized by American celebrities like Brooklyn Nets star Kyrie Irving, comedian John Oliver and actor Mark Ruffalo, whose postings against Israel went viral.

Ruffalo retracted his post accusing Israel of genocide against the Palestinians, writing it was "not accurate, inflammatory, disrespectful and is being used to justify antisemitism."

But such retractions are few and far between and the flood of antisemitic content on social media has become overwhelming.

The time for serious condemnations and action to stop antisemitism is long overdue. It must happen immediately, before the next Poway or Pittsburgh.

US President Joe Biden wrote on Twitter that "the recent attacks on the Jewish community are despicable, and they must stop" and that "it's up to all of us to give hate no safe harbor."

While these are powerful words, they came at least a week too late. Biden neglected to speak out against antisemitism for too long, perhaps because he did not want to alienate anti-Israel extremists aligned with his party who are among those responsible for the violence.

Imagine what would have happened had Biden's predecessor former US president Donald Trump not responded immediately to the antisemitic incidents. He would have faced fierce criticism, and the criticism would have been justified.

There must be zero tolerance for antisemitism, just like there is none for racism against black or Hispanic Americans or discrimination against women.

Jews should be able to go anywhere in America, feeling completely safe and wearing their kipot with pride.

My parents were rescued by righteous gentiles in Poland. The couple who saved them were officially recognized as Righteous Gentiles by the Yad Vashem World Holocaust Remembrance Center.

But as righteous as they genuinely were, even they spoke positively about Nazi leader Adolf Hitler's efforts to cleanse Poland of Jews. The Holocaust was the weakest point for the Jewish people in our history.

Now, we are at our strongest point, with the most sophisticated Jewish community since Sinai. We have a thriving Jewish state with one of the world's most powerful armies, and unfortunately, also one of the most battle-tested.

The Jewish community in America is also strong and influential, with more than 20 Jews serving in top posts in the Biden administration.

The majority leader of the Senate, Charles Schumer, is a Jew who built himself up from a humble background. He is now the most powerful Jewish elected official in America.

Perhaps he should have used that power to speak out more forcefully and to take action against extremist statements made against Israel by members of Congress.

There is so much to recognize about the accomplishments of countless Jewish Americans. But to truly celebrate Jewish American Heritage Month next year, much must be done on a local, federal and national level to stop the scourge of antisemitism.

The Algemeiner

Naftali Bennett lied his way to the top

This is not the time for Israel to be experimenting with leaders.

JUNE 8, 2021

Israel's incoming prime minister, Naftali Bennett, justified breaking his campaign promises by saying that had he kept them, Israel would be going to another election.

That lie justifying his lies proves that Bennett will not be starting his term on the right (pun intended) foot. I don't know if Bennett has a right foot, or if he ever really did. But he's responsible for bringing down the right and its iconic prime minister, Benjamin Netanyahu.

He could have joined a coalition with Netanyahu, who even offered a three-man rotation as prime minister with New Hope Party leader Gideon Sa'ar. But he preferred from day one after the election to go with the left.

Bennett promised that he would not join a government in which Yair Lapid would serve as prime minister, even in a rotation. Yet he will end up serving as prime minister in a government built and controlled by Lapid, and then under Lapid as prime minister in the unlikely scenario that the government lasts until August 2023.

"In no way will I give my hand to a government led by Yair Lapid, not in a regular way or with a rotation, because I am a right-wing man and Lapid is a man of the left and I don't sell my values," Bennett said, knowing full well that it was a lie when he said it. He has a history of being made a fool of by Netanyahu. Now it's Lapid who's doing that to him.

He promised that he would not sit in a coalition with Meretz. But its leader, Nitzan Horowitz, who said that Israeli soldiers should be on trial at the Hague, will be in the security cabinet, deciding on issues of life and death. There will also be an Arab minister in the government.

Another coalition partner, Labor, also has extremists in Ibtisam Mara'ana, who bragged about driving through the siren on Memorial Day, and Gilad Kariv, an activist Reform rabbi who is fond of provocations and J Street. Its leader, Merav Michaeli, will be the minister of transportation. Will the roads stop again on the pre-1967 border?

Bennett also promised not to join a government backed in any way by Ra'am of the Joint Arab List, and its chairman, Mansour Abbas, the leader of the Southern Islamic Movement, which is part of the Muslim Brotherhood. Now, after giving the Brotherhood a say in his policies, Bennett is calling Abbas a courageous leader and pledging billions to his pet causes in order to build a minority government.

When Bennett said, during "Operation Guardian of the Walls," that the government could not take steps that needed to be taken in mixed cities with Abbas in the government, he was absolutely right. Was he being truthful?

Bennett's party is called Yamina ("rightward"), and the people have indeed moved to the right, while Bennett has ironically moved to the left. He lost his integrity by putting his own personal good over that of the country and a majority of its people, especially his own voters.

Whom does he represent anymore? What does he stand for anymore? He and his coalition partners do not agree on anything other than hatred of Netanyahu.

It is true that Netanyahu made too many enemies over his many years in power, and Bennett took advantage of that to become prime minister. Netanyahu has mistreated the politicians who served under him and did not build up a successor who could have taken over had he decided to do the right thing and stand aside to keep the right in power, with a coalition of 80 mandates.

Perhaps the one positive from forming this government is that it could ensure that with Netanyahu removed, the right will head all governments after this one in the foreseeable future. Then again, it makes sense that the man who made Israel into the vaccination nation, kept the country safe and brought Israel peace with five Muslim countries without giving anything up should be heralded, not replaced.

The world is becoming a scarier place, and Israel needs Netanyahu more than ever to deal with it. How will Israel tell the world not to go back to the terrible Iran deal if its own foreign minister, Yair Lapid, supported it? How will Israel deal with the challenges of Joe Biden's administration without the man that the U.S. president calls "my friend, Bibi"?

This is not the time for Israel to be experimenting with inexperienced leaders.

Bennett and Lapid announced that they'd formed a government half an hour before the deadline. Had the deadline passed, there would have been three weeks in which a right-wing government could have been formed to avoid another election.

But going to an election is certainly preferable to having a left-wing government that the people of Israel clearly did not want the last time they went to the polls. In the final analysis: Sooner or later, a fifth election is inevitable.

The Jerusalem Post

Jews need to be united on a united Jerusalem

Throughout the history of the Jews, in good times and bad, one issue that has united Jews across every spectrum has been the fate of Jerusalem.

NOVEMBER 13, 2021

The World Jewish Congress's esteemed president, Ronald Lauder, spoke about the need for unity among the Jewish people at WJC's Theodor Herzl Awards Gala on Tuesday at the Museum of Modern Art in New York.

The event honoring Pfizer CEO Dr. Albert Bourla, whose parents were among a small number of Holocaust survivors from Thessaloniki, Greece, was purposely held on the anniversary of Kristallnacht, the 1938 "Night of the Broken Glass," in which more than a thousand German and Austrian synagogues were attacked, Jewish-owned businesses were looted and 30,000 Jews were jailed.

"We are at a crossroads that is dangerous for the Jewish people," Lauder warned at the event, justifiably.

As a son of survivors myself and a member of the United States Holocaust Memorial Council, I am deeply concerned about the future of the Jewish people, amid rampant antisemitism, chasms in the American-Jewish community and pressure on the Jewish state that the Holocaust proved so necessary.

Throughout the history of the Jewish people, in good times and bad, one issue that has united Jews across every spectrum has been the fate of Jerusalem. Even at times when the Jewish people have been extraordinarily divided, united Jerusalem has united us. This must be seen as one of those times.

Currently, the Biden administration is pressuring Prime Minister Naftali Bennett and Foreign Minister Yair Lapid to enable the reopening of an American consulate serving the Palestinian Authority in the heart of downtown Jerusalem. This would be an unprecedented step – enabling a diplomatic mission to serve a foreign entity in another country's capital.

At a Jerusalem press conference last weekend, Bennett and Lapid both ruled out surrendering to such a demand. But Biden wants his campaign promise on the matter to be fulfilled at all costs, to the point that he could potentially make such a move unilaterally and illegally, against Israel's will.

This is the time for the entire American-Jewish community to unite to keep Jerusalem united, because Biden's move is about a lot more than the consulate.

The Abraham Accords came from then-president Donald Trump making clear that there is no daylight between Israel and the US. He emphasized that lack of daylight with every step he took, from renouncing the dangerous Iranian nuclear deal, to recognizing Israeli sovereignty over the Golan Heights to formally recognizing united Jerusalem as Israel's capital and moving the US Embassy.

Reopening the US consulate for the PA would be a destructive step on the way to undoing other moves courageously undertaken by Trump for Israel, America's closest and most loyal ally. It would be a sign that the Biden administration is purposely creating daylight with Israel again.

It is understandable that the Biden administration would want to harm the Abraham Accords, which were an unprecedented accomplishment initiated by the president's predecessor from a rival party. But it would be completely short-sighted and would distance Middle East peace after significant progress was finally made.

This move would isolate Israel in the international community and return to the intransigent Palestinian leadership the veto power that enabled them to quash all peace overtures by Democratic and Republican presidents and secretaries of state in the past. It would also harm chances of formally expanding the Abraham Accords to other countries, most notably Saudi Arabia, which was active behind the scenes in efforts to advance Middle East peace during the Trump administration.

The diverse Israeli government, which is divided on most issues, is united in favor of expanding the Abraham Accords, so failing to do so by refocusing diplomatic energies on the Palestinians again would be a tremendous missed opportunity.

Israel desperately wants to reach out to the Biden administration, to Democrats and to self-proclaimed progressive American Jews. As part of that effort, Lapid and Finance Minister Avigdor Liberman said this week that they want to immediately proceed with a plan to change the status quo at the Western Wall, which would ignite tension.

Lapid listed several reasons why implementing the Kotel plan was important to him, including improving relations with Diaspora Jews. But the truth is that changing the status quo at the Kotel would divide both Diaspora and Israeli Jews at a time when we can least afford disunity.

Israel must refrain from taking such a divisive step at such a sensitive time.

Like the Israeli government, the American-Jewish community needs to understand what is at stake and present a unified front around keeping Jerusalem united and properly advancing peace in the Middle East.

The Jewish Press

Ensuring the Abraham Accords

NOVEMBER 19, 2021

Throughout the history of the Jewish people, in good times and bad, one issue that has united Jews across every spectrum has been the fate of Jerusalem.

Even at times when the Jewish people have been extraordinarily divided, united Jerusalem has united us.

This must be seen as one of those times.

Currently, the Biden administration is pressuring Prime Minister Naftali Bennett and Foreign Minister Yair Lapid to enable the reopening of an American consulate serving the Palestinian Authority in the heart of downtown Jerusalem. This would be an unprecedented step – enabling a diplomatic mission to serve a foreign entity in another country's capital.

Bennett and Lapid both ruled out surrendering to such a demand at a Jerusalem press conference on Saturday night. But Biden wants his campaign promise on the matter to be fulfilled at all costs, to the point that he could potentially make such a move unilaterally and illegally, against Israel's will.

This is the time for the entire American Jewish community to unite to keep Jerusalem united, because Biden's move is about a lot more than the consulate.

The Abraham Accords came from then-President Donald Trump making clear that there is no daylight between Israel and the U.S. He emphasized this with every step he took, from renouncing the dangerous Iranian nuclear deal, to recognizing Israeli sovereignty over the Golan Heights, to formally recognizing united Jerusalem as Israel's capital and moving the U.S. Embassy.

Reopening the U.S. consulate for the PA would be a destructive step on the way to undo other moves courageously undertaken by President Trump for Israel, America's closest and most loyal ally. It would be a sign that the Biden administration is purposely creating daylight with Israel again.

It is understandable that the Biden administration would want to harm the Abraham Accords, which were an unprecedented accomplishment initiated by the president's predecessor from a rival party. But it would be completely short-sighted and would distance Middle East peace after significant progress was finally made.

This move would isolate Israel in the international community and return to the intransigent Palestinian leadership the veto power that enabled them to quash all peace overtures by Democratic and Republican presidents and secretaries of state in the past. It would also harm chances of formally expanding the Abraham Accords to other countries, most notably Saudi Arabia, which was active behind the scenes in efforts to advance Middle East peace during the Trump administration.

The diverse Israeli government, which is divided on most issues, is united in favor of expanding the Abraham Accords, so failing to do so by refocusing diplomatic energies on the Palestinians again would be a tremendous missed opportunity.

Israel desperately wants to reach out to the Biden administration, to Democrats and to self-proclaimed progressive American Jews. As part of that effort, Lapid and Finance Minister Avigdor Liberman said this week that they want to immediately proceed with a plan to change the status quo at the Western Wall, which would ignite tension.

Lapid listed several reasons why implementing the Kotel plan was important to him, including improving relations with Diaspora Jews. But the truth is that changing the status quo at the Kotel would divide both Diaspora and Israeli Jews at a time when we can least afford disunity.

Israel must refrain from taking such a divisive step at such a sensitive time.

Like the Israeli government, the American Jewish community needs to understand what is at stake, and present a unified front around keeping Jerusalem united and properly advancing peace in the Middle East.

The Jerusalem Post

Diaspora Jews should at least be let into Israel

125 years later, Jews around the world are once again in distress, this time, because the state that Herzl helped create is closed off to them.

JANUARY 1, 2022

Zionist visionary Theodor Herzl wrote in The Jewish State in 1896 that his plan for a state for the Jewish people was "conditioned on the motivation of the distress of the Jews" around the world.

Unfortunately, 125 years later, Jews around the world are once again in distress, this time, because the state that Herzl helped create is closed off to them.

I normally visit Israel three or four times a year, and I haven't come since February 2020, immediately before the COVID-19 pandemic intensified and changed the world.

But there are countless stories that are much sadder than mine: Mothers who missed their daughter's wedding, children who missed their parent's funeral, and grandparents who have not met their grandchildren.

As heart-wrenching as all these stories are, perhaps they would be understandable if Israel had decided to isolate itself completely and end all entrances into the country by air, land and sea.

That is not the case. Israel decided to allow only those who have an Israeli passport into the country.

In making that decision, Israel decided to differentiate between Moshe who lives in Modi'in and his cousin Moshe who lives in Manhattan.

Why? Is one Moshe more committed to the Jewish state than the other? Why is Moshe's residence and citizenship the only criteria?

The rationale for Israel's existence is to be a haven for the Jewish people. The laws should be the same for Jews who live in Israel and abroad.

Israel's current policy sets a bad precedent. What would happen if there was another international tragedy, like a nuclear strike? Would Israel decide to be a haven for some Jews and not others?

The government of Israel is also pushing away Diaspora Jews, who have every right to be offended. We support Israel, we fight for Israel where we live, and we teach our children to love Israel. It is harder to teach that commitment when the Jewish state is shunning us.

This is the worst possible time for Diaspora Jewry to be cut off from Israel. The plagues of intermarriage and antisemitism need to be tackled with the positive messages of Jewish pride and peoplehood that a trip to Israel provides better than any other remedy.

Young people especially need to learn the importance of Israel. But the Birthright Israel program has been handicapped for two years. A top travel company that had 43 buses of Birthright participants in December two years ago had only three this year.

Visits to Israel are desperately needed for Diaspora Jews of all streams, no matter what their level of affiliation.

At a meeting of the Knesset Foreign Affairs and Defense Committee on Monday, United Torah Judaism MK Israel Eichler asked Foreign Minister Yair Lapid why Diaspora Jews were not allowed into the country. Lapid's response was disingenuous.

Lapid told Eichler that the reason Israelis are allowed to come in is that it is possible to track them by phone and to know where they live. Lapid said this was not true of Jews who live abroad.

Excuse me? Is Israel no longer the StartUp Nation? Why can they not take our telephone number or give us some kind of device that can be tracked?

An idea raised by Religious Zionist Party MK Simcha Rothman makes a lot more sense. He said Israel should let in zaka'ei shvut – people eligible to make aliyah under the Law of Return.

Implementing this idea would justify continuing to temporarily turn away non-Jews who want to visit the country while permitting in Jews, for whom Israel remains a haven.

It would not be discriminatory, just as the Law of Return is not discriminatory. It is merely a recognition of the role that Israel has played since its founding. And it would correct the mistake that Israel is currently making.

It is wrong for Israel to decide to be a state of all its citizens, as the Joint List party wants it to be. Even Ra'am (United Arab List) MK Mansour Abbas has recognized that "The State of Israel was born as a Jewish state, and it will remain one."

Being a Jewish state is a responsibility. Israel is currently shirking that responsibility and not living up to Herzl's vision.

The Jerusalem Post

Netanyahu, sign the plea deal to help save the world

An American Jewish perspective on the proposed plea agreement.

JANUARY 19, 2022

As we speak, opposition leader Benjamin Netanyahu is in the process of deciding whether to accept a plea agreement from the prosecution that would require him to plead guilty to some of the charges against him and leave politics.

He is making this decision together with his attorneys and his family, and it is his absolute right to do what he sees fit for his future. As well, he is undoubtedly considering the good of the country and the impact his decision will have on internal Israeli politics.

But there should be more to it. Netanyahu should also take into account the bigger picture and the wider world. With all due respect to the narrow parliamentary and political issues he must deal with as Israel's opposition leader in the Knesset, there are bigger fish for him to fry.

Now, the world is in desperate need of the guidance of an elder statesman. Freed of his responsibilities as Likud leader and Knesset member, Netanyahu can take that role. Netanyahu could go to the Iran-deal talks in Vienna and speak to relevant parties, without the burdens and complications of officially representing Israel. He can go to America whenever he wants, without getting permission to miss votes and the Knesset ethics committee asking who funded his trip.

When there are elections between a pro-Israel candidate and an anti-Israel candidate anywhere around the world, he could provide a superstar endorsement that would make a difference. In particular, the American Jewish community requires a mentor at this time of divisiveness, and concerns about the coronavirus, antisemitism, security and alienation from Israel. Netanyahu can provide his prominent voice, talents, experience and intelligence.

As one of the world's most eloquent statesmen and most successful politicians in history, he would earn a pretty penny as a speaker, consultant and adviser to corporations, organizations and even countries. Isn't that better than wasting millions on lawyers for a trial that could take years?

As a veteran lawyer, I know anything can happen in litigation. The innocent can be proven guilty for all sorts of reasons and technicalities. A long trial with hundreds of witnesses is a waste of time for someone of Netanyahu's stature. Whatever the charges are against Netanyahu, they pale in light of greater issues Israel and the world are facing.

Members of the current government have said they want Netanyahu to reject the plea deal, because the opposition is stronger without him. The Likud has not been able to form a government, because Netanyahu has too many enemies. As well, it is also because they obviously fear losing the glue that keeps the government together.

The moment he leaves the scene, the Right can come back to power immediately and a government that can only unite in its dislike for Netanyahu can be toppled. Israelis can get the kind of government that an overwhelming majority of them want.

The prosecution, which knows it can also lose in court, needs to be more flexible in reaching a deal. The standard seven years a politician is distanced after conviction for a serious crime in Israel should not be necessary for what Netanyahu allegedly did. Two or three years should be enough to achieve their goal of setting an example.

But who knows? Even if it does end up being seven years, maybe Netanyahu could return to power at age 80 and lead Israel for another decade. His father, Prof. Benzion Netanyahu, continued working into his late 90s and died at the age of 102.

For all those reasons, Netanyahu should sign the deal.

The Algemeiner

Ruth Calderon is unfit to head the Jewish Agency

The former Yesh Atid MK has engaged in hate speech throughout her career, and no one has asked her to take it back.

JANUARY 31, 2022

When Israel embarked on "Operation Guardian of the Walls" following massive rocket fire from Hamas in the Gaza Strip in May, the country needed national unity.

Then-Prime Minister Benjamin Netanyahu received full support for the operation from Naftali Bennett, who would shortly thereafter become his successor, and from other anti-Netanyahu politicians, such as current Finance Minister Yair Lapid and Finance Minister Avigdor Lieberman. Even United Arab List (Ra'am) Party head Mansour Abbas went to a synagogue that had been vandalized by Arabs and pledged to rebuild it.

Only a real extremist, fringe politician would come out against the government when Israel Defense Forces are fighting terrorists, while both Jewish and Arab civilians are running for cover. Only the most divisive Israeli would post a message on Facebook denouncing the operation.

And she did.

Who would go so far as to attack a prime minister that way in the heart of a war, while lives were being lost?

A woman currently running for a position seen as no less than the presidency of the entire Jewish people in Israel and around the world: chair of the Jewish Agency for Israel.

Former Yesh Atid Party Knesset member Ruth Calderon became Alternate Prime Minister Lapid's candidate to head the Jewish Agency after Yesh Atid minister Elazar Stern put his foot in his mouth and joked about shredding sexual harassment complaints in the IDF. Stern has actually defended women's rights throughout his military and political careers, but he was still forced out of the race for suggesting that he might have done otherwise.

Calderon has engaged in hate speech throughout her career, and no one has asked her to take it back. Luckily for her, she has never criticized women's rights. Calderon only attacked Orthodox Jews.

In 2015, soon after she was not re-elected to the Knesset, she issued a scathing attack on Orthodox MKs for not supporting her radical bills about Shabbat, civil marriage and shmita.

"It was the religious population that stopped me," she complained. "Their closed-mindedness, their libeling and their cruelty will collapse the dream of a national home for the Jewish people in the Land of Israel."

Anyone who would say that about any group of Jews is unfit to hold a post once held by Zionist visionary Theodor Herzl.

Calderon also called for ending the Orthodox monopoly on burial ceremonies, which is a fringe point of view even among the most secular Israelis. She spoke out against Lag B'Omer, a holiday that crosses ethnic and religious divides.

Bennett endorsed Stern, but he declined to go along with Lapid's shift to Calderon, undoubtedly because of her unconventional approach to Judaism. Many were outraged by a video of Calderon saying on a panel with former Jewish Agency chairman Avraham Burg that she puts bread—not matzah—on her Seder plate in order to remember the poor.

"Not Jewish Agency material," has been a frequent comment from many who viewed the clip.
If there ever was an understatement, that's it. Mansour Abbas would be a better fit to head the Jewish Agency because he at least makes an effort to be a unifying figure.

The Jewish Agency needs to unite the very divided Jewish people, which is a formidable task, but it can be done, and it has been done.

I wrote the first article supporting Isaac Herzog even before he officially ran for Jewish Agency chairman, even though his views on many issues look different from mine and he may not at first blush observe as many commandments as his grandfather, the late chief rabbi of Israel. Clearly, Natan Sharansky was also a unifying figure that the Jewish Agency needed.

If there ever was a time when bonds within the Jewish community need to be strengthened, it is now, when the plagues of COVID-19 and divisiveness have joined intermarriage and anti-Semitism in harming us disproportionately around the world. All streams need to work together.

There are currently multiple candidates being considered by the selection committee. None may be a Herzog or a Sharansky, but understand the need for Jewish unity and peoplehood, and can make an effort to fight the aforementioned plagues.

The selection committee is set to meet on Tuesday and perhaps will make its final choice ahead of the Jewish Agency Board of Governors meetings at the end of February. Lapid is pushing the committee hard to adopt his choice, telling them that he will become prime minister and the Agency head will have to work with him.

But events of the last two weeks have underscored that anything can happen in Israeli politics and Lapid rotating into the Prime Minister's Office is far from a foregone conclusion. The selection committee needs to resist political pressure and pick whoever could best serve the Jewish people and, as importantly, the Jewish Agency.

I hope and pray that the committee rejects Calderon and chooses a unifying figure.

The Jerusalem Post

It's wrong to eulogize World Mizrachi

MK Meir Porush declared World Mizrachi dead in a Knesset speech attacking Prime Minister Naftali Bennett and MK Mansour Abbas.

FEBRUARY 14, 2022

It has been nice to see my World Mizrachi movement join the esteemed company of Yankees legend Joe DiMaggio, Pope John Paul II, Israeli professor Amnon Rubinstein and writers Mark Twain and Ernest Hemingway.

But I wish it was not for being the victim of incorrect and premature eulogies.

For his own political reasons, United Torah Judaism MK Meir Porush declared World Mizrachi dead in a Knesset speech attacking Prime Minister Naftali Bennett and United Arab List (Ra'am) MK Mansour Abbas. As reported in The Jerusalem Post, Porush said Abbas would soon no longer "be the boss" and would "disappear, just as World Mizrachi Movement disappeared."

"The [Mizrachi] movement, which Bennett holds in high regard, is based on mixed classrooms, mixed youth movements," Porush said. "Bennett's government is based on hybrid movements that put nationality above religion, but we all know the Mizrachi movement fell off the political landscape."

Porush is correct that Mizrachi is not affiliated with any of the parties in the current Knesset. It was affiliated for decades with the National Religious Party, which became Bayit Yehudi, which, unfortunately, for technical reasons, did not end up fielding candidates in last year's election. He is wrong when he suggests that the movement puts nationality over religion.

Clearly, the impact of Mizrachi and religious Zionism is felt more than ever now in Israeli politics and countless other spheres of influence in Israel and around the world.

The same prime minister whom Porush attacked, Naftali Bennett, is the former controversial head of Bayit Yehudi and the first prime minister to wear a kippah. His closest ally, crocheted-kippah-wearing Religious Services Minister Matan Kahana, inherited his ministry from Shas and has embarked on controversial, far-reaching reforms of the way kosher certification and conversions are conducted in Israel. For better or worse, there is no gainsaying that the movement has been influential.

Religious Zionists are to be found in almost every political party. Israel's first female ambassador in London, Tzipi Hotovely, is a proud religious Zionist whose first diplomatic experience was as a successful emissary of Bnei Akiva in Atlanta. She served as an MK from the Likud. There are crocheted-kippah-wearing diplomats representing Israel across the globe.

World Mizrachi is an umbrella organization whose US constituents include Amit, Emunah, Religious Zionists of America and several Bnei Akiva-related organizations.

In World Zionist Organization politics, World Mizrachi has delivered unprecedented achievements, most notably Avraham Duvdevani heading Keren Kayemeth LeIsrael-Jewish National Fund, a body that was dominated for decades by the Labor Party. While he is not from Mizrachi, the head of the WZO and interim chairman of the Jewish Agency is Yaakov Hagoel, another proud religious Zionist.

That brings us to the other eulogy on the pages of the Post, in an article by Daniel Goldman titled "Will haredim take control of Israel-Diaspora relations?"

Goldman wrote about the WZO's new Eretz Hakodesh faction and the rise of haredim (ultra-Orthodox) in international Zionist institutions that they previously boycotted.

"This new interest in Diaspora politics will change the dynamics that have existed up until now," Goldman wrote. "The group most threatened by this within the WZO and Jewish Agency are World Mizrachi. The presence at the caucus launch of both the Orthodox Union and Yeshiva University (the latter participating silently) should be of concern to the leaders of World Mizrachi. Both of these hugely important religious institutions have traditionally formed part of the Mizrachi coalition within the national institutions. A possible shift towards the haredi faction could undermine their position."

One must commend Rabbi Pesach Lerner of Eretz Hakodesh for spearheading efforts to galvanize haredi support for Israel in Zionist institutions for the greater good. He could be a welcome partner for World Mizrachi, which remains the second-largest faction and one of the most influential factions in the WZO.

The truth is that, unlike in Israel, it is sometimes hard to distinguish between haredim and religious Zionists in America, where the constituencies often overlap within the Orthodox community without rancor.

World Mizrachi remains the thriving global movement it has been for 120 years, with a presence in thousands of communities around the world, uniting the people of Israel with the values of the Torah and Land of Israel and influencing Israel's future in nearly all walks of life.

As for current politics, there has never been a better time for our movement to take some time off. While the prime minister may arguably be one of us, he came to power in a questionable manner, and he is taking steps that have definitely divided religious Zionists.

The conversion issue, for instance, is extremely complicated and pits very respected rabbis such as Rabbi Eliezer Melamed, who is normally seen as hardline, against Chief Rabbi David Lau, who is normally seen as moderate. It raises different issues in Israel and the US, and is probably best dealt with, if at all, by Mizrachi's independent constituent organizations.

Similarly, America is suffering from one of the most divisive eras in its history. There are strong views among religious Zionists on both sides of the aisle, and enhancing that rift now would be counterproductive.

Religious Zionists were dragged into Israeli politics in the United Kingdom last week, which resulted in misunderstandings, apologies and avoidable problems.

This is the time when it is best for World Mizrachi to speak in a unifying voice for religious Zionists around the world and temporarily remain above the fray.

Soon enough, Mizrachi will return to playing an official, formal role in Israeli politics, as it has for decades, and as it should, in order to remain relevant and help provide Israel a better future.

As with Twain and Hemingway, even after our eulogies, the best for World Mizrachi is yet to come.

The Jerusalem Post

Iranian attack on US should wake up Israel

Iran fired 12 massive ballistic missiles at the US consulate that was being built in Erbil.

MARCH 15, 2022

The 12 massive Fateh ballistic missiles fired from Iran at the large United States consulate being built in Erbil, Kurdistan, were not only aimed at America.

They were aimed at getting all the countries negotiating a new nuclear deal with Iran to cave in to the final demands of the Islamic Republic, surrender on sanctions and enable unlimited cash to flow in, which would undoubtedly be used for similar acts of terror around the world.

Only the most feckless administration in Washington would continue negotiating after being fired upon so brazenly. If America signs a deal after that, it would become an international laughingstock, and terrorists around the world would receive a signal that they have carte blanche to act without restraint. Any remaining deterrence would be completely lost and all American servicemen stationed abroad would know that they would be cannon fodder.

The US will surprise no one when it continues negotiating with Iran, because it has proven non-stop since Joe Biden became president that it would pay any price to its greatest foes and sacrifice its greatest allies.

This is true of Ukraine, which has not received nearly enough assistance from Washington since the February 24 Russian invasion. Any hopes in Ukraine of America doing anything other than sanctioning the Russians was quickly quashed amid the rubble in Ukrainian cities. It is also true for Israel, which can only look at America's behavior in utter disbelief, dread and debilitating fear.

"Iran fired missiles at an American consulate in Iraq and yet, it continues negotiating with the same ayatollahs who fired the missiles, which would enable them to obtain a nuclear arsenal that would endanger Israel and the peace of the world," opposition leader Benjamin Netanyahu said, in a video he posted on social media. "They will remove the sanctions from Iran, which would give the ayatollahs hundreds of billions of dollars to continue such acts of terror. There is no greater absurdity than this."

Netanyahu's video will obviously have no impact on Prime Minister Naftali Bennett's government. Bennett takes pride in doing the opposite of whatever Netanyahu says to do, even when it is obvious that his much more experienced predecessor and former mentor is exactly right.

But, the attack on Erbil and subsequent Iranian claims that its real target was a Mossad facility should serve as a wake-up call to Bennett that his strategy of fighting the Iran deal from behind the scenes is a dismal failure. Israel has clearly not impacted the deal by one iota.

It is not too late for Bennett to change his dangerous and counter-productive course. His ally, Interior Minister Ayelet Shaked, said she altered Israel's five-day-old Ukrainian refugee policy, because she heard the public's feelings.

If Shaked can hear feelings, Bennett should be able to hear an enormous missile strike. He should start making his voice heard and finally raise a public alarm in Washington, European capitals and around the world, as he should have been doing all along.

In a speech in Tel Hai marking the yahrzeit of Israeli hero Yosef Trumpeldour last week, Bennett said only one sentence about Iran: "We have an obligation and a historical right to maintain our ability to protect the existence of the Jewish people and the Jewish state with our own force," he said. "We will always maintain this ability to defend ourselves by ourselves." Bennett also has a duty to address Iran's race toward a nuclear capability coherently, instead of constantly speaking in code and downplaying the greatest threat to Israel's existence.

No one in Israel is raising the alarm about Iran right now. Consequently, the issue is hardly discussed in America. Without Netanyahu coming to Congress and making noise, Israel is taken for granted, as if it is a proxy for the US. Perhaps Bennett's policy would make sense if America could be counted on, but what has happened with Ukraine has proven that America's assurances are unfortunately utterly worthless.

Due to new Russian demands, it remains unclear whether a deal will be reached. There is even talk of removing Russia from the equation to expedite an agreement.

If there is a choice between a very bad deal and no deal, undoubtedly no deal would be better. With such a bad deal, Israel would be in an untenable position, due to the money and power coming to Iran. Endowing terrorism for the foreseeable future will trump any guarantees and assurances that the Biden administration may offer to Israel as compensation.

The Saudis and the Emirates would also suffer, but the Jewish state would suffer the most. If a nuclear Iran or one of its arms, like Hamas or Hezbollah, fires a missile at Israel, its arms would be tied. That is why the missile strike on Erbil must become a rallying cry for immediate action by the US and Israel to change course and prevent that from happening.

The Jerusalem Post

Israel must say 'no' to Tom Friedman

After the Israeli government gave in to Friedman's pressure two decades ago; it is imperative for the Jewish state to maintain its security by emphatically saying no this time.

JULY 19, 2022

In February 2002, veteran New York Times columnist Thomas Friedman crossed the line from respected journalist to diplomatic adventurist, advocate, lobbyist and provocateur.

Friedman's victim was the State of Israel, which came under enormous international pressure to embark on a dangerous withdrawal from the entire biblical heartland of the Jewish people in Judea and Samaria.

The so-called Saudi Initiative, which was really Friedman's own delusion, called for a total withdrawal by Israel to the lines of June 4, 1967, and the establishment of a Palestinian state with Jerusalem as its capital. In return for relinquishing all its diplomatic, security, historic and religious assets won in the 1967 war of defense, Israel would receive an obviously empty promise that all 22 members of the Arab League would offer full diplomatic relations, normalized trade and security guarantees.

The Arab League back then still featured Saddam Hussein's Iraq, Muammar Gaddafi's Libya and Bashar Assad's Syria, who in Friedman's eyes would turn their attention from the mass murder of their own people to suddenly guarantee the future security of the Jewish state.

The world – and Friedman's own employer – should have already shunned him then as an insane purveyor of nonsense and dismissed his pathetically far-fetched ideas. But they were instead taken very, very seriously.

Ariel Sharon's Gaza Strip disengagement – and further withdrawals planned by his successor Ehud Olmert – were a direct result of Friedman's plans. The Gaza Strip withdrawal was intended to resist international pressure on Israel to relinquish land in the center of the country.

The result of this pressure on Israel, initiated by Friedman, ended up being the tens of thousands of rockets fired upon Israelis from the Strip, three avoidable wars and the overthrowing of the Palestinian Authority in Gaza by the Hamas terrorist organization. That should have been enough to silence Friedman into shame.

The final nail in the proverbial coffin of Friedman's diplomacy should have been the success of the Abraham Accords in achieving peace for Israel with four Arab countries. The accords proved that the Jewish state need not give up an inch of land, allow another capital in Jerusalem or bestow its security to a maniacal Mideast dictator. All it needed was to be strong, technologically advanced and economically successful to be a desired peace partner.

But the defeat of Donald Trump and the rise of Joe Biden unfortunately gave new life to the 68-year-old columnist, to embark on another Saudi adventure to the detriment of Israel. If Friedman had true ties in the current Saudi leadership, he would know that they could not care less about the Palestinians.

Over the weekend, while Biden traveled from Jerusalem to Jeddah, the Times published Friedman's column entitled "Only Saudi Arabia and Israeli Arabs Can Save Israel as a Jewish Democracy," in print and online.

"I suspect the Saudis will want such a game-changing moment to unfold in two stages," he wrote. Stage 1 in Friedman's new scheme is that, in return for the Saudis opening a commercial trade office in Tel Aviv, they should "demand Israel halt all settlement-building to the east of the Israeli security barrier in the West Bank and agree that the Saudi-Arab peace plan for a two-state solution be a basis of negotiations with the Palestinians."

Why Israel would adopt Friedman's failed plan from 20 years ago and harm its people in return for an unnecessary brick and mortar Saudi presence not in Israel's capital is explained as a "big psychological move." But the only psychological move is Friedman's own obsession with Israel displacing 700,000 Jews from their homes, and treating that is clearly urgent.

Stage 2 would be "the end to the Israeli occupation and a peace deal with the Palestinians," in which Israel would again bestow its security to the Arab League in return for the dubious prize of a Saudi embassy in Israel (and another one for the Palestinian state, of course).

"I can 100 percent guarantee that if the Saudis made [Friedman's proposals] public, they would play a central role in Israel's Nov. 1 election and help spark the kind of debates and creativity needed to preserve Israel as a democratic state," he wrote.

That line is the only one in Friedman's column that bears some truth. All evidence proves that if international pressure on Israel resumes, it would indeed become a key campaign issue and opposition leader Benjamin Netanyahu would win the election by a landslide.

To form a government, Netanyahu would not need the support of Israeli Arab MKs, whom Friedman also advises nefariously in his column. After Mansour Abbas's Ra'am Party joined the outgoing government on the basis of it ignoring the Palestinian issue and focusing on improving the lives of Israeli Arab citizens, Friedman urged Ra'am to instead "declare that it would only enter a Jewish-led government that agreed to negotiate with the Palestinians on the basis of the Saudi overtures."

Yes, after four elections in three years and with another on the way, Friedman is really calling for encouraging further political paralysis in Israel, just in order to advance his own rejected Mideast peace plan.

After the Israeli government made such fateful mistakes in response to Friedman's pressure two decades ago, it is imperative for the Jewish state to maintain its security – and hopes for real peace with its neighbors – by emphatically saying no to Friedman now.

The Jewish Home

Israel today pilfering from the public for pluralism

AUGUST 25, 2022

Former U.S. President Theodore Roosevelt once joked that the politicians of his time were so corrupt that "when they call the roll in the Senate, the Senators do not know whether to answer 'present' or 'not guilty.'"

Unfortunately, the same holds true in Israeli politics today.

Prime Ministers Benjamin Netanyahu, Ehud Olmert, Ariel Sharon and Ehud Barak were all investigated, Olmert went to prison for bribery, and Netanyahu is currently on trial facing charges of bribery, fraud and breach of trust.

It is possible that Israeli politicians were always corrupt, and there is just more scrutiny nowadays. Maybe it is just the system that is problematic. Perhaps our standards have risen, and our leaders must now be more careful than ever to go well beyond the letter of the law. The final option is that corruption has not increased at all, and the press and much of the public are making mountains out of molehills.

Nevertheless, if Netanyahu can be tried for accepting gifts and positive media coverage, every politician in Israel must be held to the same high standard.

It must hold true for politicians across the spectrum, not just Netanyahu and his political allies.

That is why this week's investigation of Diaspora Affairs Minister Nachman Shai and his Labor Party colleague, Knesset member and Reform Rabbi Gilad Kariv, must be taken seriously.

The investigation by Ma'ariv newspaper columnist Kalman Liebskind found that Shai had funneled 30 million shekels from his ministry's coalition allocated discretionary funds to a small non-profit organization to advance religious pluralism in Israel.

That organization, called Panim, had only two workers and a small budget, but it had Kariv as a board member until nine months after he became an MK. Panim was chosen to run the Diaspora Affairs Ministry's new Jewish Renewal Department without a required government tender.

Panim's director-general Yotam Broom is a Labor Party member and Kariv confidant who praised him on social media during his election campaign and bragged about the funding that would be given to his organization long before the decision was made officially. Broom helped the ministry form the department he would later be chosen to head.

The final revelation in the article was that the Diaspora Affairs Ministry was allowed to fund pluralism projects inside Israel, because they are deemed "societal." That preposterous decision calls into question why the ministry even exists.

It highlights the point that there is too much money coming from the State of Israel to the Diaspora, which certainly can fund itself. If Israel has more money than it needs, it should go to feeding the poor and improving housing and U.S. organizations need to rethink their fund-raising efforts.

The Reform Movement, in particular, can raise its own money instead of taking it from Israeli taxpayers. If the time has come to reverse the direction of giving to make it so Israel helps the Diaspora, it should not be for such a divisive, controversial issue within Israel.

The Kariv affair highlights the absurdity of money going from Israel to America. Conceptually, it is an outgrowth of the funding that is allocated to the religious streams which itself needs to be revisited.

It was Naftali Bennett who first changed the paradigm of Israel-Diaspora relations in 2017, when he approved a $1 million aid package from the

Diaspora Affairs Ministry he headed for the Houston Jewish community to repair the damage caused by flooding from Hurricane Harvey.

"The Jewish State is measured by its response when our brothers around the world are in crisis," Bennett said at the time.

But that was to help relieve an American Jewish community in distress due to a disaster, which should have been a very rare exception and not what 1nitiated a new rule. It should remain that the Diaspora helps fund Israel and not the other way around. And clearly the notion that Diaspora Affairs Ministry funds can be used internally inside Israel to advance a religious stream should be unimaginable.

The very fact that the government allocates discretionary funds to parties to use for their pet causes is problematic to say the least, no matter what the cause. But it may explain why Kariv did not believe he was doing anything wrong by earmarking it without prior approval.

Now that it has been proven that the Diaspora Affairs Ministry's money was allocated without following proper procedures, the allocation should be frozen immediately. Especially with an election going on in Israel, Shai and Kariv cannot be permitted to give out taxpayer money that may have been tainted.

Finally, Kariv and Shai should be given the benefit of a fair investigation while the money is frozen. They deserve to be presumed innocent until proven guilty.

But perhaps if the information in the article about Kariv had been disclosed before the race, he would not have done as well in the Labor Party primary, in which he won the third slot on the party's list as Labor's top male candidate. Labor members would have known that he gave away their tax money to an organization alleged to be myopic and even fake.

Normal process needs to be applied to determine whether Kariv can be allowed to run just as it was to Netanyahu and his former ministers Yakov Litzman and Aryeh Deri and Likud MK David Bitan.

The same rules must be applied to Kariv and Shai whose alleged crime may have been worse than the cigars Bibi accepted. Clearly, their actions could be seen as a blow to good governance, in which there cannot be two sets of rules. Their apparent behavior certainly does not foster trust in government.

Only if they will be held accountable to the same standards can Israeli politicians prove themselves unworthy of comparison to the American politicians of the Roosevelt era.

The Jerusalem Post

Why religious Zionists should vote for Smotrich

Smotrich is a man of integrity, truth and consistency. That cannot be taken for granted nowadays, after other religious Zionists in politics misled right-wing voters.

OCTOBER 24, 2022

For decades, religious-Zionist voters in Israel had a clear choice on Election Day.

Small splinter parties came and went, but it was clear that the National Religious Party, Mafdal, served the needs of religious Zionists in Israel. The Mafdal was officially affiliated with Mizrachi, which represents and unites religious Zionists around the world.

After years of political infighting over the past decade, in which parties came and went, ran in different formations and repeatedly changed their names, there is once again a clear, central address for religious-Zionist voters in Israel: the Religious Zionist Party, led by MK Bezalel Smotrich.

Smotrich is a man of integrity, truth and consistency. That cannot be taken for granted nowadays, after other religious Zionists in politics misled right-wing voters.

While those politicians compromised their values for unholy political bonds, Smotrich held true to the religious-Zionist ideals of the Land of Israel for the people of Israel according to the Torah of Israel. He deserves credit for proving he can be trusted to reject attempts to entice him and give up on what religious Zionists believe in.

Let's start with the Land of Israel. Smotrich and his candidates are fully committed to building everywhere in Judea and Samaria, the biblical heartland of the Jewish people. They have properly represented their constituency in Judea and Samaria, including residents of younger communities (that some call outposts), which need the government's support to overcome their challenges, succeed and thrive.

Smotrich lives in Kedumim in Samaria with his wife and seven children. He co-founded Regavim, an organization that monitors and pursues legal action in the court system against illegal construction by Palestinians, Bedouin and other Arabs.

"After many years, the time has come for the Right to govern for real," Smotrich says.

The Religious Zionist Party list includes other veteran residents of Judea and Samaria, including veteran Hebron activist Orit Struck and Simcha Rothman, who lives in Pnei Kedem in Gush Etzion and whose wife was raised in the largely Anglophone Neveh Aliza neighborhood of Karnei Shomron.
Encouraging aliyah from around the world

Next comes the people of Israel. Smotrich has plans for representing English-speaking immigrants to Israel and encouraging aliyah from around the world.

He recently visited religious-Zionist leaders in London and reached out to the directors of yeshiva programs for overseas students in Israel. He also took a tour of Jewish communities in the US as part of a delegation of MKs sponsored by the Jewish Agency and the Jewish Federations of North America (JFNA) that he found especially eye-opening.

"We need to maintain a dialogue with North American Jewish communities because we are a Jewish state that is the home of the entire Jewish people," Smotrich told the World Mizrachi website in an interview. "This does not mean there are no conflicts, and this does not mean there are no disputes. There are many things I disagree about with Reform and Conservative Jewry. But I understand that we are brothers. We need to speak and have a dialogue and look for common ground."

Smotrich said he maintained a connection with the leadership of the JFNA because he understands that many steps taken in Israel affect what happens overseas. In that interview, he also praised immigrants to Israel from English-speaking countries.

"This important community, which made aliyah and left behind in the US a good life, family, a livelihood and a good environment, cares about the State of Israel and the people of Israel more than about its own interests," he said. "The Anglo-Saxon community knows what Zionism is and knows what it means to pay a price for its values."

Both Rothman and Religious Zionist Party candidate Ohad Tal have vast experience working with religious Zionists around the world. Tal was an emissary in the Netherlands, worked at Israel Mizrachi and was the director-general of World Bnei Akiva.

Finally, for the Torah of Israel, Smotrich is the son of a respected religious-Zionist rabbi and attended the Mercaz Harav, Yashlatz, and Kedumim yeshivot. He spoke out against controversial plans for conversion and kosher certification in the last government and would prevent their advancement in the next one that he would join.

For the Religious Zionist Party to play a strong role in a government formed by Benjamin Netanyahu, it would need to be as large as possible. If not, Netanyahu will go in other directions, as he has in the past.

In an article published in The Jerusalem Post in February, I wrote that there has never been a better time for Mizrachi to take time off from Israeli politics.

"While the prime minister may arguably be one of us, he came to power in a questionable manner, and he is taking steps that have definitely divided religious Zionists," I wrote about Naftali Bennett. "This is the time when it is best for Mizrachi to speak in a unifying voice for religious Zionists around the world and temporarily remain above the fray. Soon enough, Mizrachi will return to playing an official, formal role in Israeli politics, as it has for decades, and as it should, in order to remain relevant and help provide Israel with a better future."

Now that Bennett is no longer in politics, that "soon enough" has come. Religious Zionists around the world can come back to taking a significant part in Israeli politics, as they always have.

I believe that supporting Smotrich and the Religious Zionist Party is the right way to do it.

The Jerusalem Post

Netanyahu needs to choose Smotrich over Biden

Netanyahu wrote in his new book that US President Joe Biden pressured him to end the war prematurely because he was feeling pressure from Congress.

NOVEMBER 21, 2022

Israel's anticipated next prime minister Benjamin Netanyahu wrote in his new book Bibi: My Story that during the May 2021 war with Hamas, he came under fire not only from Israel's enemies but also from a purported friend of the Jewish state.

Netanyahu wrote that US President Joe Biden pressured him to end the war prematurely because Biden was feeling the heat from progressive Democrats in Congress. "Bibi, I gotta tell you, I'm coming under a lot of pressure here," Biden told Netanyahu, according to the book.

Fast forward to the present. Netanyahu is reportedly coming under pressure from Washington again, this time while there is not even a war on the horizon. Biden, according to Israeli reports, is trying to preempt Netanyahu's choice for defense minister.

Netanyahu reportedly told Religious Zionist Party leader Bezalel Smotrich, who heads a list that won 10.83% of the vote, that he has been vetoed by the US.

How absurd is that?

How can the US pressure Netanyahu to ignore election results?

The issue of whether Smotrich is better suited for the finance or defense ministries is beside the point.

America is supposed to be the world's greatest bastion of democracy. How could the US pressure Israel's leader to ignore the results of a democratic election with more than a 70% turnout?

Even more absurd are the reports that Netanyahu caved into that pressure from Biden, or at least used it as leverage to avoid giving the independently minded Smotrich a key post that he would rather give to a loyalist, or even better, a yes-man who would allow Netanyahu to run the ministry himself.

The pressure from Washington should have persuaded Netanyahu to do the opposite of what the Biden administration wanted. He should have announced Smotrich's appointment as defense minister that very day.

Smotrich received the endorsement of the Israeli electorate that pronounced him qualified for a top post by giving his list 14 seats. He is a rising star who should be embraced, not shunned, by the prime minister.

Netanyahu must realize that when the Biden administration fires at Smotrich, its real target is the incoming prime minister himself. By delegitimizing the only possible government in Israel, they are trying to overthrow Bibi before he has even gotten a chance to take the oath of office.

Biden and other top former Obama administration officials never forgave Netanyahu for his March 2015 speech in Congress against the Iran deal. The anti-Israel State Department has had a clear grudge against Netanyahu for decades. The leaks about State Department figures not liking Israel's election results should surprise no one.

The attempt to dictate the composition of Netanyahu's cabinet is nothing short of diplomatic revenge and must not be tolerated. It is also not new.

I am old enough to remember when American administrations excoriated newly elected prime minister Menachem Begin and declared future prime minister Ariel Sharon persona non grata.

So now their targets are Smotrich and Otzma Yehudit leader Itamar Ben-Gvir, who are both being vilified before being given an opportunity to govern. Along with Netanyahu, they were the clear winners of the Israeli election, even if the Biden administration would have voted for someone else.

The vote empowered the Religious Zionist Party and the religious Zionists that the party represents. The party's electorate was young, indicating that its support will only grow in years to come.

There are a record number of kippah-wearers in the Knesset. This is the wave of the future, and the Americans cannot ignore this trend nor attempt to suppress it.

Not for the first time, the administration in Washington is guilty of cultural relativism. I don't see the State Department undermining democracy in Finland or telling French President Emmanuel Macron whom to appoint to his cabinet.

The Biden administration has no right to interfere, and its top officials who have dealt with Israel for years should know that it would backfire. If Netanyahu gives in to the Biden administration now, when the next war takes place, he should not be surprised to see that America will no longer be standing behind him.

The Jerusalem Post

Jewish American organizations endorsing antisemitism must be denounced

The IHRA working definition of antisemitism was widely adopted - the pro-Israel community should use it to target obvious antisemites.

DECEMBER 22, 2022

Once upon a time, identifying an antisemite required the proverbial duck test. If it quacked like an antisemite, then it probably was an antisemite. But there were still ways for antisemites to duck responsibility.

That has changed in recent years, due to the International Holocaust Remembrance Alliance's (IHRA) uniform working definition of antisemitism, which has been adopted by 38 countries, including the United States, by executive order in Donald Trump's White House, three years ago.

That definition of antisemite is a perfect fit for Congresswoman Ilhan Omar, a Democrat from Minnesota, one of the first two Muslim women (along with Rashida Tlaib) to serve in Congress. Her actions in recent years directly match several of the clauses of the definition.

Omar has used symbols and images associated with classic antisemitism when she tweeted that "Israel has hypnotized the world" and that US politicians' support for Israel was "all about the Benjamins," a reference to hundred dollar bills. Even the Democratic House leadership, led by outgoing Speaker Nancy Pelosi (D-CA), said when she invoked that canard that Omar had "engaged in deeply offensive antisemitic tropes."

Another part of the IHRA's definition of antisemitism is "accusing Jewish citizens of being more loyal to Israel." She clearly did that in February 2019, when she angered fellow House Democrats Eliot Engel and Nita Lowey (both of NY) by saying "I want to talk about the political influence in this country that says it is OK for people to push for allegiance to a foreign country."

Omar has also repeatedly applied double standards toward Israel and singled out the world's only Jewish state for her own political reasons. She even equated Israel and the US with Hamas, Afghanistan and the Taliban. Nevertheless, despite all that quacking, several left-wing groups in the US still have the audacity to pretend that Omar is not a duck.

Who came to Omar's defense when House Minority Leader Kevin McCarthy (R-CA) pledged to remove Omar from the House Foreign Affairs Committee? J Street, Ameinu, Americans for Peace Now, Bend the Arc: Jewish Action, Habonim Dror North America, New Israel Fund, T'ruah and the Religious Action Center of Reform Judaism.

"As Jewish American organizations, we oppose Republican Leader Kevin McCarthy's pledge to strip Representative Ilhan Omar of her House Foreign Affairs Committee seat based on the false accusations that she is antisemitic or anti-Israel," the organizations wrote in a joint statement, last week. "We may not agree with some of Congresswoman Omar's opinions, but we categorically reject the suggestion that any of her policy positions or statements merit disqualification from her role on the committee."

The groups unabashedly added that their support for Omar "seems especially exploitative in light of the rampant promotion of antisemitic tropes and conspiracy theories by [McCarthy] and his top deputies, amid a surge in dangerous right-wing antisemitism."

All these fringe groups must be condemned for endorsing an antisemite. Their claims to be pro-Israel should no longer be taken seriously by anyone of repute. Just like the pro-Iranian protesters of Neturei Karta, it must be made clear that they do not represent American Jewry. To their credit, unlike the Reform leaders who endorsed Omar, at least the Neturei Karta are honest about their feelings toward Zionism.

AIPAC, the American Israel Public Affairs Committee, rightfully criticized J Street for its Omar endorsement. "J Street says it's a 'false accusation' to call Rep. Ilhan Omar anti-Israel," AIPAC posted on

Twitter. "A false accusation? J Street is defending one of the most vocal anti-Israel critics in Congress."

While it is important to maintain a big tent of varied pro-Israel movements, these groups must be seen as crossing the red lines disqualifying entry into the tent. Clear criteria must be crafted that would, of course, forbid supporting a blatant antisemite.

There is no doubt the overwhelming majority of Reform Jews would be in that tent, even if their current leadership would not. The Religious Action Center of Reform Judaism should devote more action to educating Reform Jews and less fighting against Israel in Congress.

Why is it not obvious that to be a pro-Israel organization means taking steps to enable the most important House committee for Israel to have one less vote against it? That is why Kevin McCarthy needs to be praised for not only speaking out but also being ready to double down and take immediate action to help Israel.

McCarthy, who is facing a tough race for Speaker of the House next month, deserves the support of pro-Israel Congressmen, who should ensure he obtains the 218 votes typically needed to become speaker of the 435-member body. If for whatever reason McCarthy is not chosen, whoever becomes House Speaker must ensure that Ilhan will not be on the Foreign Affairs Committee.

This is the time for truly pro-Israel organizations to speak out. Condemning Omar is not about politics, it is about getting the real pro-Israel community's ducks in a row and targeting an obvious antisemite.

The Jerusalem Post

Netanyahu's Israeli gov't must stop coddling Qatar

Netanyahu should insist that the US start following the anti-Israel money from Doha to Gaza and to campuses influencing academia throughout the US, thus causing tremendous, incalculable damage.

JANUARY 30, 2023

The new government of Prime Minister Benjamin Netanyahu has been described by American media as a right-wing extremist, hardline, ultra-hawkish and the most far Right in Israel's history.

Nevertheless, last Thursday, on a night when Israeli citizens were forced to spend the night in bomb shelters due to indiscriminate rocket fire from the Gaza Strip, Israel's neophyte Foreign Minister Eli Cohen, who is learning on the job, issued unconscionable praise for Qatar.

Cohen thanked the Qataris for enabling members of Israel's national beach volleyball team to participate in a tournament in Doha, after previously threatening to prevent them from receiving visas and keep them out of the country.

"In sports and on the playing fields, there is no place for boycotts and exclusion," Cohen wrote. "I hope this is another step toward bringing our nations closer together."

The words in Hebrew for volleyball is kadur af, which also means flying bullet. There is important symbolism in the double meaning of the word.

The Qatari regime supports the Hamas terrorist organization that rules Gaza and facilitates its terrorism against Israeli civilians. Qatar still pumps money into terrorists' hands with Israel's knowledge and bewildering acquiescence.

The Netanyahu government turns a blind eye to the shipments of dollars from Doha to Hamas in Gaza. The time has come for Netanyahu to stop the arrival of these suitcases full of protection money supporting terror.

The same Qatari regime helps fund the Boycott Divestment and Sanction (BDS) efforts against Israel around the world and professorships for anti-Israel lecturers at top American and British universities teaching the future leaders of the US and United Kingdom.

Thankfully, Saudi Arabia has stopped similar behavior in recent years. But Israel and the rest of the world continues to turn a blind eye to Qatar, even allowing the regime to host the World Cup, which was used as a propaganda event for the Palestinians. Israeli journalists, who also required the help of their Foreign Ministry to enter Qatar, were shamefully mistreated at the tournament.

The world needs to start asking: If Qatar has so much disposable money to put on a lavish show for the World Cup, for international diplomatic warfare against Israel and to spend on American and British campuses, why does Doha not build a university for Palestinians in Gaza?

After all, top American universities, including Northwestern, Georgetown and Carnegie Mellon, have large campuses in Qatar that receive massive funding from Doha. There are also Qatari branches of top universities in London, Paris, Munich and Calgary.

US Secretary of State Antony Blinken is set to arrive in Jerusalem on Tuesday for talks with Netanyahu. He is expected to warn Israel against taking steps to strengthen its legal system; initiating construction for residents in Judea and Samaria; and facilitating Jewish prayer at Judaism's holiest site, Har Habayit (the Temple Mount).

Blinken's tweet about preserving the status quo at what he called "the Haram al-Sharif/Temple Mount," following a visit to the site by National Security Minister Itamar Ben-Gvir, did enough damage.

There is no better time for Netanyahu to deflect such harmful and unnecessary pressure on America's top ally in the Middle East by highlighting the havoc caused by Qatar around the world.

Netanyahu should insist that the US start following the anti-Israel money from Doha to Gaza and to campuses influencing academia throughout the US, thus causing tremendous, incalculable damage.

When Cohen meets with his American counterpart, instead of praising Qatar again, he must raise the question of why no one is looking into Qatari money and insisting on transparency. He should ask why America relies on fickle regimes like Doha and Ankara that end up backstabbing the US time and time again.

Only if the Israeli and American governments and the leaders of the international community stop coddling Qatar, can the Abraham Accords move forward again in a serious manner. Standing up to Qatar will create an atmosphere that would enable more Arab and Muslim countries to gain legitimacy for normalizing relations with Israel.

That in turn would make the world realize that Netanyahu's government is striving to achieve peace in the Middle East, and is not so hawkish, hard-line and extremist after all.

The Jerusalem Post

Are the Abraham Accords proving to be a success?

The UAE merely needs the security and safety that can ensure its stability and enable the Emiratis to pass on what they've achieved to the next generation. There could be no better ally for the US.

MARCH 9, 2023

Strategic Affairs Minister Ron Dermer and National Security Adviser Tzachi Hanegbi recently returned from what could end up being a fateful trip to Washington, where their aims were stopping the nuclearization of Iran and expanding the Abraham Accords.

Biden administration officials have reportedly warned Israel in recent weeks that America may not end up advancing these two key issues because they are upset at Prime Minister Benjamin Netanyahu's government for its policies on construction in Judea and Samaria and its legal reform plan.

But the truth is that it is not the actions of Israel that are harming the expansion of the Abraham Accords but the inaction of the United States.How did the US help with the Abraham Accords?

The role of the US in the accords was to bolster the security of Israel's partners. That American commitment faced a key test when Iranian-backed Houthi rebels in Yemen fired several strikes on Abu Dhabi in January and February 2022.

The UAE needed the help of the Americans, who they assisted in past wars in Afghanistan, Iraq, Kuwait and Saudi Arabia. They were left sorely disappointed by the US, whose response was both too little and too late. It took seven weeks for the US to react, which is unacceptable for an ally.

The US has also neglected its commitment to provide the UAE with the advanced Lockheed Martin F-35 Lightning II combat aircraft, citing bureaucracy and other excuses. America insisted on vetoing when the planes would be used, a violation of the Abraham Accords.

After America failed to keep its promises to the UAE, why would Saudi Arabia or any other potential Abraham Accords partner trust the Biden administration? Such countries would only take risks to join if the US is seen as reliable, consistent and having their back.

America's failure to honor its commitments only drives the UAE closer to a variety of potential strategic partners, including China and even Iran. This strategic diversification happened primarily because the US has lost its bearings with what should have been a critical strategic ally.

On a recent visit to Dubai, I was told by Emiratis that the UAE justifiably feels betrayed by America, which it hoped would be its most important strategic ally.

By contrast, since the accords were signed in Washington in September 2020, the Israelis and their partners in the United Arab Emirates, Bahrain and Morocco have honored their commitments in the agreements. Unlike the US, Israel was there for the UAE immediately after the attacks.

Trade has skyrocketed among the four countries and Israelis have been coming en masse to visit Dubai, Abu Dhabi, Manama and Marrakech. More than 400,000 Israelis have visited the UAE. Trade between Israel and the UAE reached $2.59 billion (NIS 9.3 b.) in 2022, an increase of some 124% from the year before.

According to a 2022 report released last month by the Abraham Accords Peace Institute, total trade between Israel and its new regional partners reached $3.57 b. (NIS 13.5 b.) in 2022, up from $1.095 b. (NIS 3.9 b.) in 2021 and $593 million (NIS 2.1 b.) in 2019.

It is also in America's interest to deliver on its promises of security to the UAE not only because of its wealth and infrastructure but because of its energy that the US may need. UAE President Crown Prince Mohamed bin Zayed Al Nahyan should be looked up to as a model to the world for his country's economic success and philosophy of tolerance, modesty and educational reform.

Due to that successful leadership, the UAE does not need America's money, unlike other countries in the region. It merely needs the security and safety that can ensure its stability and enable the Emiratis to pass on what they've achieved to the next generation. There could be no better ally for the US.

This was not the first time America let the UAE down. After their service in Afghanistan, the Emiratis were not even told when the US decided to pull out. The US asked the UAE to take in America's Afghan interpreters and they are still safely in the UAE.

Finally, America has also disappointed the UAE and the region by not doing enough to stop Iran from building its nuclear program and even blocking European attempts to instill new sanctions on Iran. America's policy on Iran remains unclear to the UAE and the region.

Hopes had been raised by the US joining Israel in their largest joint long-range military drill last month that preceded sabotage strikes on a couple of Iranian nuclear facilities. Those actions led to optimism that after its own attempts to reach a deal failed, the Biden administration was slowly admitting that Prime Minister Benjamin Netanyahu was right on Iran and Barack Obama was wrong. Iran's military support for Russia's war with Ukraine and merciless crackdown on its own courageous protesters finally made the Democrats see the merit of Netanyahu's warnings.

It has been reported that US Ambassador to Israel Thomas Nides thankfully told a meeting last month that there will be no more negotiations with Iran during Biden's presidency. Whether or not Iran talks return to America's agenda, the US needs to further get its act together and treat the UAE with the loyalty that it has earned and deserves.

Now is the time to ensure that the UAE receives what it was promised by Washington in the Abraham Accords, complete security, and thereby enable the expansion of peace in the Middle East.

Israel National News

Interview

From normalization to education.

MARCH 14, 2023

Martin Oliner, co-President of Religious Zionists of America (RZA) and Chairman of the Center for Righteousness and Integrity, and Reva Oliner, President of the Center for Righteousness and Integrity, speak to Israel National News after spending several weeks visiting Arab states, including Oman, Bahrain, Abu Dhabi and Dubai.

In Oman, the Oliners met with ministers, including the deputy foreign minister, in meetings arranged by B'nai B'rith. They were part of a small delegation of less than 10 people.

They spoke to the deputy minister about air rights for Israel. "He said they were considering it and lo and behold, a few days later Israel was granted the air rights," Reva says.

"We were able to get a good feel for them," Martin says. "We had our wish list. I think they knew what our wish list was and we were glad to see that all this could happen so quickly after our visit."

He adds that a few years after the signing of the Abraham Accords, their impact can be felt economically.

"Israel has benefited to the billions and they in turn likewise have seen 400,000 Israelis come to Abu Dhabi and Dubai," he says. "But in a certain sense, the feeling that we got in the area and the question is: Would the Abraham Accords be doable today? Could they be accomplished? And I would think that it would be very difficult."

He adds that he does not believe Oman opening its airspace to Israel will lead to further success with the Abraham Accords.

"I think that the neighborhood that would normally come aboard will not come abort in today's environment," he says. "I think it's fair to say that both Bahrain and Abu Dhabi Dubai are very disappointed in the results of the Accords. I don't think they've gotten any of the benefits they were supposed to."

According to him, as economic success stories, the Gulf states today are mainly concerned with security and maintaining what they have achieved. He notes that part of the Abraham Accords was a promise of delivery of F-35s, along with increased protection from their ally, the United States, which did not pan out the way they had hoped.

"I think they believe that the United States is an important partner…but I think what they've decided and what the feelings that we get is that they're disappointed with the United States who has been their main ally for all these years," Martin says. "Now why do they need a main ally? So that they continue in safety and security."

He explains that while they were in Dubai they had an "extraordinary" meeting at the Ritz-Carlton Hotel.

"I was privileged to host a program on the Culture of Peace. The Culture of Peace is designed to bring together what the Emiratis and what the Accords are all about: bringing about peace. What we're trying to do is get different organizations together. We were successful in bringing together Trends, which is leading UAE Think Tank, the Sheik of Peace from Iran, who was very well known, people from Italy, people from the United Nations, people from Azerbaijan, from all over the world, to come together for a program that will ensure that we actually create a curriculum [including textbooks] for the culture of peace. That's the biggest problem we have today."

Speaking of the messages coming from the Biden administration regarding the internal policies in Israel, he comments that he believes they are taking their cue from left wing American Jewish groups.

"I don't think the problem is the United States government," he says. "I think the problem is that there are those who focus on Israel differently and who believe that they should have the last say, not even that they should come here and vote like the democracy that Israel is. But I think many feel that they're above Israel, because of contributions they've made over the years, or for whatever reasons."

He continues: "Regrettably, the [American] Jewish Community today is untutored, uneducated, growing more and more with assimilation. So it's not like there's a traditional group that once represented a large percentage of Jews that's out there that's vibrant. That group has shrunk and continues to shrink. The largest group of Jews today are those that are totally unaffiliated and that's where the problem is."

According to him, the problem is that American Jews see the protests going on in Israel surrounding judicial reform and they are concerned but they don't actually know what judicial reform is about.

Speaking about the possibility of a rift between the diaspora and Israel, he notes there are different issues and problems faced by Jews inside and outside of Israel.

He mentions antisemitism as the greatest problem facing American Jews today but it's not really a problem in Israel, and also the US trend of increasingly high intermarriage rates.

He has also been expanding an enormous effort on Jewish education. He mentions that haredi schools in Israel need to begin teaching English and STEM (science technology, engineering and mathematics) subjects at a young age.

But he also stresses that a major issue facing Israel currently is a "problem that no one wants to speak about."

"The community that's [non-observant] and totally uneducated [on Judaism] and has no idea about their background, that community consists of about over a million people today, and why should they be here [in Israel], why should they not [emigrate]? The solution is only in education. Again, not forcing religion. But remember, Jewish history is part of the [Bible]. The Bible is the Jewish history and that culture needs to be imbued in everyone."

The Jerusalem Post

How not to make peace between Israel and Saudi Arabia

I don't even think Biden can make peace with Netanyahu, his supposed friend for decades, who he has been snubbing unnecessarily for more than seven months.

AUGUST 1, 2023

When the Abraham Accords were brokered by the Trump administration between Israel and the United Arab Emirates, I wrote in this newspaper about how they had set a new paradigm for peacemaking in the Middle East that would be much more successful.

Attending the White House ceremony in which the accords were signed and my visits to the UAE, Bahrain and Morocco have underscored the success and viability of the accords.

"This agreement with the UAE is the first of what will become the new trend," I wrote three years ago. "Instead of land for peace, from now on, Israel will be trading peace for peace. Israel will no longer relinquish land and evacuate Jews from their homes in return for calm and instead receive rockets, terrorists' tunnels and suicide bombers in return. The Palestinians will have to overcome their internal divisions, their corruption, and their misplaced priorities, or they will be rightly forgotten."

I wrote that none of the concessions Israel made for decades led to the Palestinians reciprocating. Rather than make the concessions necessary to help their own people, Abbas and other Palestinian leaders stalled for time, resorted to violence and incitement, and missed countless opportunities.

"This agreement should be a wake-up call to the Palestinians that no one is waiting for them to overcome their stubbornness anymore," I wrote.

"Whether they like it or not, those days are now officially over. Their ability to hold Israel hostage has been lost forever."

In hindsight, I admit I was wrong.

There are at least two people who are still waiting for the Palestinians, enabling their stubborness, and are not only willing but genuinely excited about the prospects of holding Israel hostage: Current American President Joe Biden and his top adviser on the Middle East, New York Times columnist Tom Friedman.

Biden and Friedman have clearly learned nothing from decades of failure to achieve peace by forcing Israel to make concessions that would put the Jewish state in peril. They have turned a blind eye to the success in peacemaking of former president Trump, who was able to think outside the box and wisely reject those who told him that there was no other way.

Biden told his reelection contributors on Friday that a deal may be on the way with Saudi Arabia – after talks his national security adviser Jake Sullivan had with Saudi officials in Jeddah – aimed at reaching a normalization in relations between the kingdom and Israel.

He didn't say what the deal would entail. But he doesn't have to, because he has Friedman for that.

"I believe that, at a minimum, the Saudis and Americans could (and should) demand four things from Netanyahu for such a huge prize as normalization and trade with the most important Arab Muslim state," Friedman wrote after meeting with Biden.

These four things are: An official promise not to annex the West Bank – ever; not to build new West Bank settlements or to expand existing settlements; no legalization of "wildcat" Jewish settlement outposts; and transferring some Palestinian populated territory from Area C in the West Bank (now under full Israeli control) to Areas A and B (under Palestinian Authority control) – as provided for in the Oslo Accords.

Friedman ended his column with what may have been seen as a joke at the time: "If it also forced Netanyahu to abandon the extremists in his cabinet and make common cause with the Israeli Center-Left and Center-Right, well, wouldn't that just be the cherry on top?"

Now it is clear that Friedman was not kidding. This is actually Biden's plan.

He wants to overthrow the current Israeli government and replace it with a coalition he would like better, with Yair Lapid and Benny Gantz taking the jobs of Bezalel Smotrich and Itamar Ben-Gvir. He doesn't care about making peace between Israel and the Saudis. He wants to make war with the Israeli voters who elected a right-wing government.

Anyone who understands Israeli politics knows there is no chance for this. Lapid and Gantz will not suddenly become Bibiphiles, even if it means Israel making peace with the entire Arab world. Gantz said it himself in English in June.

The Times of Israel reported that during an event at the Washington Institute for Near East Policy, Gantz was asked whether his party would be willing to swap out Smotrich and Ben-Gvir in the coalition in the event that an agreement is signed with the Saudis. Gantz said his faction would not join the government but would act as "strategic backup" from the opposition benches.

"I think peace is always a good trend for the State of Israel, and if it needs my backup for that, it will get my backup for that, but I will not get into this government," he said.

But Friedman doesn't care. He wrote about how he told the president in the White House that a US-Saudi mutual security pact that would involve Saudi Arabia normalizing relations with Israel depended on Israel making concessions to the Palestinians that would preserve the possibility of a two-state solution.

He admitted that he warned Biden that if he made a deal without a significant Palestinian component, "it would simultaneously strike a death blow to the Israeli democracy movement – by giving Netanyahu a huge geopolitical prize for free after he just did something so antidemocratic – and to the two-state solution, the cornerstone of US Middle East diplomacy."

"It would spark a rebellion in the progressive base of his party and make ratification of the deal well nigh impossible," he also admitted warning the president.

So now the cat is out of the bag. Not only can there be no peace agreement between Israel and Saudi Arabia using the successful strategy of the Abraham Accords that left the Palestinians and their intransigence out, Biden and Friedman are now giving veto power over any possible deal to the Palestinians and their allies in Congress.

No, Netanyahu and Saudi Crown Prince Mohammed bin Salman Al Saud will not be allowed to decide the terms of a peace agreement between their countries. Biden and Friedman will put the likes of Ilhan Omar and Rashida Tlaib in charge.

These developments have only persuaded me even more that I have been right in saying for three years that no agreement will be reached on expanding the Abraham Accords as long as Biden remains president.

The Saudis just don't trust America under Biden, who came to Saudi Arabia from Israel and couldn't even get the Saudis to lower the price of oil ahead of an American midterm election. The Biden administration can't even broker normalization between Saudi Arabia and the US, which is an obvious prerequisite for him to deliver a deal with Israel.

I don't even think Biden can make peace with Netanyahu, his supposed friend for decades, who he has been snubbing unnecessarily for more than seven months.

Peace is not around the corner between Israel and Saudi Arabia, and it's not because of Netanyahu, Smotrich, or Ben-Gvir. Netanyahu has made peace with three Arab countries, and he is willing to go far to broker a Saudi deal.

Speaking to Fox News last week, Netanyahu said a Saudi deal would "be a pivot of history. It will effectively end the Arab-Israeli conflict and enable us to end the Palestinian-Israel conflict."

But Netanyahu added a dose of reality in the interview that I hope Biden watched from the White House. He said he has long believed that Israel must first make peace with the Arab world and only then with the Palestinians.

"The Palestinians, who refuse to recognize Israel in any boundary, are only 2% of the Arab world," Netanyahu said. "If we make peace with the other 98%, the Palestinians will stop believing that one day the broad mass of the Arab world will destroy or dissolve Israel, and that will bring them into a more realistic position."

If Biden had done the right thing and invited Netanyahu to the Oval Office instead of Friedman, he would know the truth. Instead, he is unfortunately doing everything to prove that he does not know how to make peace between Israel and Saudi Arabia.

The Jerusalem Post

Will Israel, Jewish world be less polarized in the Jewish New Year?

Both sides need to decide on their own now that there will be no more victories of one side over the other and that key decisions on Israel's future will have to be made by consensus.

SEPTEMBER 18, 2023

As the new year 5784 begins, it is important to learn the lessons of what made 5783 one of the most divisive years in Jewish history.

That is saying a lot, of course, because the Jewish people have been around for nearly 4000 years. As Jerusalem Post senior commentator and former executive editor Amotz Asa-El revealed in his recent book The March of Folly, there have been no less than 12 civil wars in the history of the Jewish people.

There have been disputes nonstop through Jewish history. The Ethics of Our Fathers (Pirkei Avot), offers guidance about how best to resolve them. "Every dispute that is for the sake of Heaven, will in the end endure, but one that is not for the sake of Heaven, will not endure," the text says.

The example given of a dispute for the sake of heaven is that of Hillel and Shammai, whose camps were constantly at odds but respected and deferred to each other. Hillel was quoted as saying in Ethics that lessons must be learned from Moses's brother Aaron, who "loved peace and pursued peace."

The peace referred to here is not with the enemies of the Jewish people but our own internal divides. Fast forward to the current dispute in the Jewish state over Prime Minister Benjamin Netanyahu's government's legal overhaul. Proponents and opponents of the deal have made their voices heard in the Knesset, in the streets of Israel, and cities around the world, and now in the Supreme Court.

The plan's opponents scored a victory before the 25th Knesset left for its first recess in March. Its proponents won a victory of their own before the Knesset left for its current recess in July.

Both sides need to decide on their own now that there will be no more victories of one side over the other and that from now on, key decisions on the country's future will have to be made by consensus.

The Left should have learned that before it forced through the ill-fated Oslo diplomatic process whose 30-year anniversary has been marked this month. The Right has been learning the limits of its power since an exclusively right-wing government was sworn in last December.

Tuesday's televised proceedings at the Supreme Court presented the strong views of both sides. The negotiations that took place behind the scenes concurrently give hope that long awaited compromises can finally be reached soon.

For those talks to bear fruit, they should be conducted quietly, out of the public eye, and at the highest levels trusted by both sides. Mutual recriminations in public by Netanyahu and his current main political alternative Benny Gantz do not accomplish anything. They need to respect each other like Hillel and Shammai, not spar on TV.

Netanyahu was right to expedite compromise efforts ahead of a meeting with US President Joe Biden in New York during the United Nations General Assembly. But he should have taken into account other Americans long ago – namely the Jewish community in the US.

American Jewry is extremely divided now, dragged into Israel's hyperpolarization over judicial reform. To be frank, we American Jews already had our share of internal rifts before, and we didn't need another hot potato.

It was the plan's opponents who dragged us in – organizing protests across America from the Brooklyn Bridge to the Golden Gate Bridge. Even if the demonstrators meant well, the protests have made Israel look terrible, creating a tremendous hillul Hashem (desecration of God's name.)

Many American Jews who intended to visit Israel as the 75th birthday of the Jewish State has been marked canceled their plans due to the negativity surrounding the dispute. We anxiously await the disputes being settled in Israel, so we can have an easier time getting along in America.

It is time for Netanyahu, Gantz and other Israeli political elites to set aside their differences or make way for less stubborn leaders who can. I openly endorsed Bezalel Smotrich and his Religious Zionist Party on the pages of the Post before the last Israeli election. As an American Jewish leader, I faced criticism for taking that step.

It has been my friend Simcha Rothman of Smotrich's party who has been the driving force pushing the legal reforms through the Knesset. Rothman, who chairs the Knesset Constitution, Law, and Justice Committee, has had his share of successes, and he has had his share of failures.

I have told him that I believe the time has come to stop fighting and begin compromising. I say that now here to his political opponents as well.

The time has come for both sides to act like Aaron, Hillel, and Shammai. That means making a serious effort at pursuing internal peace that – with God's help – will endure and will enable 5784 to be a better and a more united year for Israel and the Jewish people.

The Jerusalem Post

What is Israel's endgame in Gaza?

There must be a paradigm change, because if not, what is the point of risking the lives of Israel's impressive soldiers and the reservists who left lucrative jobs to fight for the country?

OCTOBER 11, 2023

After the horrific acts of merciless barbarism against innocent Israeli civilians perpetrated by bloodthirsty Hamas terrorists on Simchat Torah, it is hard to write looking forward and not back.

As this is being written, tens of thousands of IDF soldiers are stationed near Gaza, ready to enter. Israel's security cabinet has met multiple times and made decisions that have remarkably not been leaked to the press. Chances are that the ministers were briefed about the IDF's operational tactics and targets. But has anyone decided the actual goals of the war?

Strategic Affairs Minister Ron Dermer, the minister closest to Prime Minister Benjamin Netanyahu, spoke generally about his government's objectives in an interview with CNN's Dana Bash on Sunday, a day in which he attended security cabinet meetings and was on the phone when US President Joe Biden called Netanyahu. "We need to cripple the capacity of the terrorists," Dermer said, without revealing too many details.

What does that mean?

We obviously don't know.

But we know it means a very different end result than all other wars and operations in Gaza that ended up with Hamas completely uncrippled.

It means there will be a change in the paradigm, because if not, what is the point of risking the lives of Israel's impressive soldiers and the reservists who left lucrative jobs to fight for the country?

Here is an important suggestion: the IDF needs to craft a security zone around the Gaza Strip to prevent future infiltrations. The security zone would be no man's land and would not enable additional surprises.

It was not safe to have communities so close to the Gaza Strip that has been controlled by terrorists since the 2007 Hamas takeover. Such a security zone would obviously not stop rocket attacks, but it would give the Iron Dome missile defense system additional precious seconds to protect people.

Israel has had security zones on its border before, including in Lebanon. A security zone on the Lebanese border can be restored.

During the time the security zone is in place, international efforts must be made to inculcate a culture of peace in the next generation of Gazans and eliminate a culture of terrorism.

Dermer spoke about how Iran initiated the war in an effort to "scuttle a historic breakthrough in the Middle East."

It is interesting that after betting pools were created on whether the potential agreement between Israel and Saudi Arabia would be sabotaged by Israel, the Palestinians, or Biden, it ended up being Iran.

Biden, of course, did his part, too.

The Wall Street Journal reported Sunday that Iranian security officials helped plan Hamas's attacks after authorizing them at a meeting in Beirut last Monday.

The Biden administration admitted on Saturday that there was "no doubt" Tehran has been providing support for Hamas in the form of funding and arms, the Journal reported.

What connects these two reports is that the Biden administration has enabled Iran to receive access to billions of dollars that were frozen in South Korea. It also distributed hundreds of millions of dollars in US taxpayer funds to the Palestinians.

Internal documents obtained by the Washington Free Beacon in August found that despite internal assessments that such funding could boost Hamas, the Biden administration allocated the money anyway. The internal documents included the draft of the exemption request and internal emails about the need for the Treasury Department to grant it.

"We assess there is a high-risk Hamas could potentially derive indirect, unintentional benefit from US assistance to Gaza," the State Department wrote in a draft sanctions exemption request circulated internally in March 2021, shortly after Biden took office, according to the report. "Notwithstanding this risk, the State believes it is in our national security interest to provide assistance in the West Bank and Gaza to support the foreign policy objectives."

The Biden administration must acknowledge its role in facilitating the worst terrorist attacks on Israeli soil in the 75-year history of the Jewish state.

It must make up for this strategic error by giving full support to Israel to do everything necessary to ensure that Hamas and Islamic Jihad will never be able to attack Israel again from Gaza, Judea, or Samaria.

Finally, Biden must seek a deal between Israel and Saudi Arabia along the parameters of the Abraham Accords, with no Palestinian involvement or concessions to the corrupt Palestinian Authority or the terrorist organizations.

That would prove that lessons have been learned from mistakes. Moving forward while never forgetting the atrocities of October 7, that should be the end game of the war in Gaza.

The Jerusalem Post

The failure of US Jewish leadership Antisemitism is only getting worse across the world, including in Israel

NOVEMBER 27, 2023

October 7 will go down in history as the most colossal failure and worst surprise in the history of the State of Israel.

Recognizing the enormity of the disaster, the IDF chief of staff and the heads of Southern Command, military intelligence, and the Shin Bet Security Service have already prepared resignation letters that they intend to submit soon after the end of the war in Gaza.

Prime Minister Benjamin Netanyahu has been criticized for not doing the same.

But has anyone called for the resignations of the leaders of the top Jewish organizations in the United States?

I will not be calling for them to quit either. But serious questions must be raised.

Were American Jewish leaders not caught similarly off guard by a dangerous situation that had been bubbling beneath the surface that they had been ignoring for too long, with disastrous results?

Could anything not have been done to prevent the startling rise of antisemitism? Could the scary situation on American college campuses not have been averted?

Netanyahu has rightly been slammed for facilitating the transfer of suitcases of money to Hamas. Did American Jewish leaders similarly facilitate money going to causes that have undermined the safety of American Jewry?

Perhaps before October 7, such questions could have been dismissed as exaggerating or fear-mongering. Had I asked them at a public gathering, it is possible that eyes would have rolled and no proper answer would have been given.

But here we are on what Bret Stephens rightly wrote in The New York Times must be seen as a perpetual October 8. Every single day after the most catastrophic day in Israel's history must be devoted to righting its wrongs. We cannot afford to move on until the policies of American Jewish groups that were proven so dangerously incorrect are changed dramatically.

Jewish Federations, Hillel groups, and the Anti-Defamation League in particular must reconsider their priorities, programming, and alliances.

Did they veer too much away from helping American Jews in need in order to adopt universal causes? Did they go too far in criticizing Israel for its internal policies and proposals that only showed the vibrancy of Israeli democracy?

Such questions can also be asked of individual American Jews, too many of whom gave money to Black Lives Matter, colleges, and universities and now regret it. Some even gave money to charities that once helped Jewish immigrants and now facilitate the integration of immigrants who will make American policies less pro-Israel over time and lay the seeds for antisemitism.

Tikkun Olam (the Jewish concept of fixing the world) sounds great on paper. But now it is the fixing that needs immediate fixing.

It is becoming increasingly clear that intersectionality is not helpful to the Jewish people.

Polls showing support for Hamas and opposition to Israel among Americans, especially among young adults, prove we are losing an important battle and the situation is out of control. Prior to October 7, it was unimaginable that in America there would be so much support for Hamas and that Jewish power in the US could be so diminished.

Just as the Jewish state has failed its population in the critical mission of ensuring that there would never be a day justifiably comparable to the Holocaust, so too have American Jewish organizations failed the people they purport to serve.

Every Jewish organization in the United States needs to refocus and reconsider what it is trying to accomplish.

People came to the November 14 "March for Israel" in Washington with different motives. Some came because of Israel and the just war that it is fighting. Some came because of the unbearable antisemitism experienced since October 7. Some came because of the unabashed complicity of university administrations with Hamas supporters and their failure to protect Jewish students on campus.

No one could have imagined the full extent of antisemitism that existed in the United States. Organizations that fight antisemitism and the constituent organizations of the Conference of Presidents of Major American Jewish Organizations must acknowledge that they did something wrong if unmasked antisemitism has gotten this bad.

We knew that the governments of Qatar and Saudi Arabia were pouring tons of money into American universities, yet, like the missiles fired from Gaza and Lebanon, we thought the problem would just go away. Meanwhile, millions of young minds have been corrupted and taken hostage.

Now we must wage war against antisemitism. A window of opportunity following the atrocities of October 7 is quickly closing.

Just like Israel must destroy Hamas – and ideally, other proxies of Iran – while it has sufficient support in the United States, American Jewish organizations must act before the tide turns completely against us.

And just like, in Israel, groups that bitterly fought each other have abandoned their platforms and united against a common foe, we American Jews must unite in an unprecedented effort to turn our horrible failure into the success that we so desperately need for our future.

The Jerusalem Post

10 Lessons for a Better 2024

JANUARY 2, 2024

In the Talmud's tractate Megilla, Abayei says the reason we read about the Jewish people's curses before Rosh Hashanah is so that the curses will be contained in the year that we are leaving behind.

The wisdom of the Talmudic sage is evident as we depart from 2023, the worst calendar year for Israel and the Jewish people since the Holocaust.

It was a year in which both Israelis and Diaspora Jews fought too much internally until our enemies reminded us – as they have throughout history – that we have no choice but to remain united.

It was a year in which both Israeli and American Jewish leaders were surprised by devastating dangers bubbling beneath the surface that they had been ignoring for too long, with disastrous results.

It was a year in which both Hamas and antisemites in the United States (and all over the world) stopped hiding their genocidal intentions and revealed them with pride and no shame.

Now that year is finally over, we are entering a year that, while we pray will be much better for Israel and the Jewish people, could still turn out to be even worse if wrong decisions are made.

Here are 10 lessons that must be learned to ensure a better 2024.

1. **Our enemies mean what they say**: When the leaders of Hamas tell the sympathetic international media that they want to initiate more October 7s until Israel is destroyed, they are very serious. Three Israeli prime ministers over the past few years acted under the assumption that Hamas wanted to cooperate with Israel in helping Gaza economically, so they facilitated Qatar's billions going to Hamas and increased the

number of Gazan workers entering Israel. From now on, we will act upon what our enemies do and say, not our own wishful thinking.

2. **Defeat Hezbollah to prevent October 7 on steroids**: The firepower of Hezbollah dwarfs that of Hamas, which not only got away with massacres inside Israel but has also managed to keep Israel at war for three months. If they can do that without precision missiles targeting Israel, imagine what Hezbollah can do with 150,000 missiles and rockets, including guided missiles ready to strike the most sensitive military and civilian targets in Israel.

Hezbollah must be eliminated or its missiles destroyed to end an existential threat to Israel when it is already weakened from war. The best way to prevent Hezbollah and Hamas from attacking Israel again is to sanction Iran effectively. Jewish organizations must pressure the world for necessary economic sanctions against Iran, the adversary that funds attacks on the US by the Houthis and others.

3. **Condition reconstruction on "educational reconstruction"**: The entire world will want to see Gaza rebuilt in the year ahead. But Israel holds the key to facilitate the reconstruction and must not permit it without parallel educational reconstruction. Israel must use its leverage to insist that the people of Gaza are taught a curriculum with a culture of peace and tolerance, which was part of the basis of the Abraham Accords.

The failures of UNRWA, which taught Gazan children to hate Jews and worship martyrs, cannot be allowed to be repeated by the international community when Gazan kids go back to school after war.

4. **Insist on ending antisemitic policies on campuses**: Following the shameful antisemitism displayed by the presidents of three top American universities, there is finally momentum toward ending discriminatory policies that have harmed Jewish students for decades.

The time has come for the elimination of diversity, equity, and inclusion (DEI) programs on campus that have encouraged antisemitism and have gotten out of control: While other bigotry is not tolerated, antisemitism has been permitted. The top US Jewish organizations must make restoring a meritocracy in American higher education the cornerstone of their strategy for the year ahead, a lesson learned from their past failures which have been revealed by the unfortunate surprises following October 7.

5. **Stop Qatar from dictating policies and selecting professors in the US:** While antisemitic tropes about Jews controlling universities with money are false, that accusation is actually true of Qatar, which annually gives Hamas hundreds of millions and allocates billions to America's top universities. Cornell University, where my grandson courageously stands up for Israel, received $1.8 billion to open a medical school in Qatar. Qatar uses its money to dictate university policies and who teaches students their narratives about the Middle East. Tenure for faculty must be eliminated while the federal government takes action to revamp the system before it is too late.

6. **Zero tolerance for holding our cities hostage:** The pro-Hamas protests in New York, Los Angeles, and Chicago have been treated with kid gloves, as if antisemitism is a justified reason to paralyze America's largest cities. They began after theft in stores in inner cities became tolerated. The masked hoodlums who have closed highways near our airports must be arrested and significantly punished before they become role models for uninformed college kids who attend pro-Hamas protests on campus without knowing where the river and the sea are located. The antisemitic protests will spread across America and spiral out of control if a heavier hand is not dealt immediately.

7. **Don't accept Israel as an excuse for hating Jews:** There has always been open hatred of Jews in America from both fringes, but traditional Judeo-Christian values have always been the American way. What is happening now is that unabashed antisemitism has entered the mainstream, with Israel being used as an excuse. Israel is not a reason for antisemitism, it is merely a symptom. In the 75 years after the Holocaust it was held at bay but no longer. The IHRA definition of antisemitism includes holding the average Jew in America accountable for Israel's policies. This can no longer be allowed to be socially acceptable. We are

at a crossroads that could result in Jews no longer feeling welcome in the US unless action is taken immediately.

8. **Teach America about the danger of antisemitism.** Antisemitism has been around since the first Jew, Abraham, was thrown in a fiery furnace by Nimrod; and Esau hated his brother Jacob. Google searches for "kill Jews" are up 1,800%; "Hitler was right" up 120%; and "why are Jews bad" up 450%. American children must be taught the dangers of the oldest form of discrimination, which is also the most prevalent in America. Antisemitism cannot be eradicated but it can be dealt with constantly and effectively to practically learn lessons from the Holocaust. This could increase deterrence against hatred of Jews before kids arrive on campus.

9. **Make Israel education the basis for a bar-mitzvah:** Jewish students arrive on college campuses nowhere near ready to defend Israel and confront antisemitism. Just like we don't send our kids into a dangerous neighborhood in an inner city, we need to recognize the dangers of campuses. Israel education must begin way before Birthright Israel. It must be compulsory for bar and bat-mitzvah students in synagogues of every religious stream in the US, from Reform to Haredi, from Los Angeles to Lawrence, to Lakewood. In most Reform and Conservative synagogues, leverage over the kids to learn who they are ends with their party at 13, so inspiring Israel education must become a prerequisite for the party.

10. **Improve Jewish education in Israel, too:** While it is true that more Torah is being learned in the Land of Israel than at any time in history, there are also more uninformed Jews than ever.

The atrocities of October 7 that did not differentiate between the most religiously observant and secular Israeli Jews should inspire a Jewish reawakening. If being Jewish is a reason to be murdered, Israelis uneducated about Torah Judaism must seek out why it is also a reason to live. Non-coercive and inspiring education must be offered in the secular education stream and entertaining adult education programs should spread in secular communities across Israel.

If all of these lessons are learned and implemented, perhaps 2024 will be remembered as the year when blessings began and the curses finally ended.

Israel National News

Interview: 'We are paying the price for twenty years of neglect'

There must be a paradigm change, because if not, what is the point of risking the lives of Israel's impressive soldiers and the reservists who left lucrative jobs to fight for the country?

FEBRUARY 25, 2024

Martin Oliner, chairman of the Center for Righteousness and Integrity, spoke with Arutz Sheva - Israel National News about the state of antisemitism in the world today.

"We are having a redundancy of antisemitism throughout the world. Forty-eight years ago president Haim Herzog tore up the most violent resolution, in a speech that made it clear that racism and Zionism have no connection. This very week, the United Nations has imposed a similar farcical resolution on all of us, and that farce continues. The antisemitism that he experienced has grown by leaps and bounds, beyond anyone's imagination."

He focused first on the October 7th massacre: "That antisemitism has not changed at all. It's amazing that some of the folks who live on the border, despite all of their suffering, have still not recognized that their friends across the border are not their friends. We've tried to make as much peace as possible, and seen only bullets and more bullets and more bullets.

He then addressed antisemitism in the USA: "Antisemitism in Israel and antisemitism in America share one common aspect - everyone involved who should have and did know enough to thwart that antisemitism has really fallen down in so many different ways. It's hard to believe that when your enemy tells you that they're going to kill you, but when they plant 150,000 missiles in the south or 200,000 in the north - they don't mean business?"

"In America, we've known for years that the Qataris are putting billions of dollars into the universities. They spent over $2B in the last three or four years indoctrinating a misconception about what education is about. In Queens, New York , there are maps where Israel doesn't exist and eighth graders are taught about Palestine."

He discussed the situation in northern Israel: "I believe that 1701 is not a solution. Israel has to strike as soon as it's ready. Whether Nasrallah strikes first or not is irrelevant. It has to get done. Unfortunately, we have to pay the price for twenty years of neglect."

He also laid out his plan for 'the day after' the war in Gaza: "When we rebuild Gaza, we must make sure that there is a culture of peace, that we raise a generation where our children and our grandchildren don't face similar problems. Hate is being taught at every level, and any kind of re-establishment has to be conditioned on an education change. It has to be a culture change at every level."

He specified one particular aspect of confronting the many challenges that Israel faces: "There should not be a notion of resilience for the north or south. Israel must adopt an all-hands emergency position of unity. There is no room in Israel today for anything but a clear picture of what needs to be done. All American organizations need to get together to work, and that is how we're going to resolve this."

The Jerusalem Post

Antisemitism is only getting worse across the world, including in Israel

It will be a challenge, but I pray that the people of Israel will remain united against our enemies and defeat them in Israel and around the world.

MARCH 4, 2024

Nearly 50 years ago, then-president Chaim Herzog tore up an antisemitic resolution at the United Nations that declared Zionism to be racism. Proving how little has changed since then, were it not for a United States veto, the UN Security Council would have passed a farcical antisemitic resolution on February 20, 2024.

Antisemitism has only intensified in Israel and around the world and it is unfortunately only going to get worse.

Let's start with Israel. Every infiltration, murder, rape, and kidnapping on October 7 was an act of antisemitism. So are all the 13,000 rockets fired from Gaza since then and every missile and drone launched from Lebanon.

The people of southern Israel are impressively resilient, but too many are still not calling out the antisemitism of their former friends in Gaza and the Arab world.

The left-wing members of the Gaza periphery's agricultural communities were proven wrong about the intentions of their neighbors on October 7. It is time to start facing reality.

Since Israel unwisely withdrew from Gaza in 2005, the only things that have not flown over the fence into Israel are doves of peace.

Many peace-pushing "doves" were incinerated in their homes on the Gaza border communities, including veteran peace activist Vivian Silver of Kibbutz Be'eri, whose remains were so burnt that it took months to identify her.

While the end to the war with Hamas may be in sight, an equally justifiable war with Hezbollah has yet to get into high gear despite emptying northern Israel of its residents for months.

Just like Israel turned a blind eye to Hamas's stockpiling of weapons that eventually had to be eliminated, the much larger arsenal in Lebanon cannot be ignored, and a war to eliminate this constant threat to Israel is inevitable. Regrettably, Security Council resolution 1701 is unlikely to succeed in disarming Hezbollah, despite our best efforts.

Hezbollah's goals are genocidal and antisemitic, and any demands from the international community that Israel sit silently with such a serious threat on its border are problematic. So is every city council resolution from San Francisco to Chicago demanding a ceasefire before the hostages come home.

The antisemitism that has reared its ugly head in the US since October 7 had been lurking beneath the surface for decades, and American Jewish leaders did not do nearly enough to stop it.

They should have seen how the students of notoriously anti-Israel Columbia University Prof. Edward Said were taking over the Middle East studies departments on campuses across the country, funded by Qatari money. Together, their followers have created a culture of antisemitism and anti-Americanism.

Now, Jewish students find themselves terrified at top American universities. Since October 7, they have faced physical violence, threats, and intimidation, and sadly, there is no end in sight.

My grandson, who headed a pro-Israel organization at Cornell, transferred from the Ivy League school to the all-Jewish Yeshiva University because he did not feel safe anymore due to the antisemitism he experienced from fellow students and teachers.

A powerful article by former Harvard Prof. Ruth Wisse published in Commentary revealed how the prestigious university's efforts to achieve Diversity, Equity, and Inclusion and other decisions have entrenched its antisemitism for many years. DEI is antisemitism and Jews are suffering from it across America. Make no mistake; as long as DEI is present, traditional university life will not be restored.

Claudine Gay was finally deposed from her post as Harvard president, but she still makes a million dollars a year as a professor. Meanwhile, the jobs of Jewish academics remain in jeopardy if they refrain from speaking out against Israel.

Jewish organizations have made alliances over decades with many progressive and liberal causes yet most of those alliances evaporated overnight on October 7 when many of the progressive groups abandoned the Jews and sided with their genocidal enemy.

When the government of Qatar decided to trump Jewish alumni donors and provide billions of dollars to universities and institutions, they felt free to exhibit their antisemitism. It is no wonder the Qataris have not been called out enough for being the sponsor of Hamas and the funders of the October 7 massacre. Their resources are unlimited and their tentacles are far-reaching.

Much like the threats from Hamas and Hezbollah, we have known about the Qatari influence for 20 years and done nothing about it; while the regime has invested trillions in antisemitism. We knew that top American universities had campuses in Doha and obtained unprecedented influence at almost every tier of education.

America must wake up and realize that Qatar is not part of the solution to any problem but the cause of too many challenging issues facing the US nowadays.

With Israel's blessing, Qatar has been giving $320 million annually to Hamas and $800 million to the Palestinian Authority (PA). Instead of revealing the extent of Qatar's brazenness to the world, the US and Israel are both making a mistake by using Qatari mediators to negotiate a ceasefire agreement. The United Arab Emirates, which normalized relations with Israel via the Abraham Accords and did not fund Hamas, would have been a much more sensible choice.

If the US and Israel do not change their course, it is unfortunately likely that the influence of Qatar and its money will only grow.

Al-Jazeera and AJ+, which are Qatari state media, will continue poisoning Western minds if they are not banished from Israel and the US, as they should have been a long time ago.

THE US must intensify its cooperation with the UAE, which changed its school curriculum to eliminate antisemitism and encourage tolerance, as mandated by the Abraham Accords.

What the UAE implemented can be a model for the essential educational reconstruction of Gaza. That process can be guided by the Culture for Peace Institute, which is dedicated to promoting understanding, tolerance, and peace among diverse cultures and communities worldwide.

It may take 20 years to inculcate a culture of peace instead of the antisemitism taught over the last 20 years. When the war ends will be the perfect time to start the process in Gaza.

Gaza's reconstruction should be conditioned on educational reconstruction because if not, more wars will take place that will result in much of what would be rebuilt coming down again.

The Abraham Accords provide a platform for educational institutions and organizations to develop programs that promote cultural understanding and appreciation. By including curricula on the history, customs, and beliefs of neighboring nations, educators can help future generations to grow up with a more open and empathetic perspective on the region's diversity.

The accords have also gone a long way toward ending the scourge of antisemitism, after Jew hatred throughout the entire Arab world was taken for granted.

It is good that Prime Minister Benjamin Netanyahu called out the antisemitism of Brazilian President Lula da Silva. But the Irish antisemitism of the last 75 years should also have been called out.

There must be zero tolerance for both kinds of antisemitism, in Israel and in America. We must expose and have zero tolerance for anyone involved in any antisemitic act, from Iran to Ireland to Brazil.

To properly fight antisemitism, we have to be united.

On my way to speak at the Knesset last week, I drove past the menorah across the street. The menorah is there because it is a symbol of unity. In the Tabernacle, it was the only item that God said had to be made from one solid piece of pure gold.

It will be a challenge, but I pray that the people of Israel will remain united against our enemies and defeat them in Israel and around the world.

The Jerusalem Post

When Schumer became his brothers' reaper

The worst part of the speech was not what made headlines. It was when Schumer threatened his brothers in Israel in a way no true guardian ever would.

MARCH 24, 2024

In almost every address to Jewish audiences throughout his decades in politics, New York Senator Charles Schumer has made a point of saying that his name means "guardian" in Hebrew and that he saw it as his duty to safeguard the Jewish people and the Jewish state.

The Democratic Party member Schumer's Middle East speech to the US Senate on March 14 was no exception. He said he very keenly felt his responsibility as Shomer Yisrael – a guardian of the People of Israel.

But that did not stop Schumer from throwing Israel to the wolves a few minutes later. With this kind of guardian, it's a good thing the Jewish state has a strong army and can defend itself.

Much has been made of Schumer saying that Prime Minister Benjamin Netanyahu has "lost his way" and encouraging Israel to initiate early elections. While inappropriate to be said by a senator to a democratic ally of the US, at least it is a legitimate point of view.

The worst part of the speech was actually not what made headlines. It was when Schumer threatened his brothers in Israel in a way no true guardian ever would.

"If Prime Minister Netanyahu's current coalition remains in power after the war begins to wind down and continues to pursue dangerous and inflammatory policies that test existing US standards for assistance, then the United States will have no choice but to play a more active role in shaping Israeli policy by using our leverage to change the present course," Schumer warned.

At a time of war, Israel needs love, not leverage – a term used only against adversaries, never about brothers. The Jewish state does not need its policies shaped from afar. It needs its allies to trust its consensus.

Schumer then added another line that started the right way yet insisted on adding an unfortunate "but" that completely contradicted the good part of the sentence.

"The United States' bond with Israel is unbreakable," he said. "But if extremists continue to influence Israeli policy unduly, then the Administration should use the tools at its disposal to make sure our support for Israel is aligned with our broader goal of achieving long-term peace and stability in the region."

So much for a guardian. Schumer put his unattainable fantasy of achieving Middle East peace above the fate of his own brothers who have suffered enough from previous diplomatic misadventures. It's like he got caught in a time warp, keeping him on October 6, while lecturing as an expert to Israelis who endured what happened the following day.

The "tools" Schumer refers to have been leaked and are known to the public: Predicating providing munitions on preventing an Israeli ground invasion of Rafah that is required to finish off both Hamas and the war. In other words, Schumer is threatening Israel that America could save Hamas out of frustration with Israel's policies.

But the scariest word here is "should," which would be no big deal if the speaker was an ordinary man offering polite advice, as in "you should tuck in your shirt." This is the all-powerful Senate majority leader, who has the ear of the president of the United States, the man who in his speech to the Senate reminded the world for the umpteenth time that he is "the highest-ranking Jewish elected official in America ever."

Based on US President Biden's praise for the speech and the leak that the administration was told about it in advance, it is likely that Biden himself sent Schumer to do his dirty work in delivering the message that "Israel is still good but Netanyahu is bad." Taking that into account this very threatening "should" is nothing short of a promise to harm Israel.

Biden used Schumer to deliver the message, like Jews have been used throughout history. Schumer could get away with it, because he has no election coming up, and when he will, the overwhelming majority of New York Jews will still vote for him.

That conversation between Biden and Schumer, in which the president got him to do his bidding, likely came after the senator delivered a speech to the AIPAC national leadership meeting three days earlier. I attended that speech, in which Schumer did not threaten Israel, insult its prime minister or make any headlines.

"I will never allow the bonds between Israel and the United States to grow weak," Schumer told AIPAC earlier this month. "The defense and security of Israel has always been one of my most important priorities ever since I came to Congress – but since October 7th, I have never been more certain that it's the right thing to do."

Schumer then called for the ousting of Hamas, not Netanyahu.

If only he had stopped delivering Middle East speeches for the week that day. But no, Schumer decided he had to become an Israeli political analyst.

"At this critical juncture, I believe a new election is the only way to allow for a healthy and open decision-making process about the future of Israel, at a time when so many Israelis have lost their confidence in the vision and direction of their government," he said. "I also believe a majority of the Israeli public will recognize the need for change, and I believe that holding a new election once the war starts to wind down would give Israelis an opportunity to express their vision for the post-war future."

Once again, Schumer started saying something, and then contradicted himself by the time he completed his thought.

So when should Israel hold an election, Chuck? "At this critical juncture" or "once the war starts to wind down?" The answer matters, because these two times are opposites.

According to all recent polls in Israel, the overwhelming majority oppose holding an election during the war, tying the hands of their leaders and paralyzing the IDF. By contrast, when the war is over, all gloves are off, and engaging in politics would no longer undermine the war effort.

When the war ends must be decided by Israeli leaders based on the recommendations from the top IDF commanders in the field, not by the Senate majority leader or even by the president of the United States. Israel has a war cabinet, in which Netanyahu makes decisions together with two former chiefs of staff in Defense Minister Yoav Gallant and his own rival for the premiership, Benny Gantz.

Together, Gantz and Gallant have more than 80 years more experience in the IDF than Schumer, so why does he not let them decide? And he does not like Netanyahu, but he, too, is a war hero, who risked his life, was injured in battle, and lost his revered older brother to enemy fire.

Netanyahu, Gallant and Gantz have their differences, which have been aired both publicly and privately. But they have managed to find a strong consensus among the people of Israel and serve them well.

It is that Israeli consensus that Schumer attacked, undermined and patronized by claiming to know better what is right for them.

Finally, in his last faulty attempt at Israeli political analysis, Schumer threatened Israel one more time.

"Of course, the United States cannot dictate the outcome of an election, nor should we try," he said. "That is for the Israeli public to decide – a public that I believe understands better than anybody that Israel cannot hope to succeed as a pariah opposed by the rest of the world."

Come on, Senator. You can't say you won't dictate and then dictate one line later.

Israel is not and never will be a pariah. Israel is defending itself from the same Islamic fundamentalist terror that attacked the United States in New York on September 11, 2001. America responded to that attack with much greater force and made much less effort to prevent civilian harm among its enemies.

If anyone is making Israel into a pariah, it is not Netanyahu, but Schumer, by highlighting and exaggerating Israel's justified actions after the worst attack on its soil in its history.

This, again, is not what a guardian is supposed to do.

Jews pray every day for the Guardian of Israel to protect the remnant of the Jewish people. Ahead of Rosh Hashanah and Yom Kippur, the Guardian is the central focus of our slihot penitential poems and prayers.

Thankfully, the guardian for whom the Jewish people pray is not Schumer but God Himself.

And He has not let us down.

The Jerusalem Post

Following Iran's attack, more US aid is needed for Israel

Israel is not only fighting for its people but for all of civilization, and this war is a must-win. That costs money, too.

APRIL 17, 2024

It was the single largest drone attack ever carried out by any country. It was the first time Iran attacked Israel directly from its own soil, after decades of relying on proxies. And it wasn't cheap.

The use of planes, Arrow missiles and the David's Sling missile defense system to shoot down more than 300 drones, cruise missiles and ballistic missiles cost somewhere between NIS 4 billion and 5 b., Brig.-Gen. Reem Aminoach, a former financial adviser to the IDF chief of staff, told the Ynet news site.

Aminoach noted that every single Arrow missile fired costs $3.5 million. He lamented that the Israeli Treasury was holding up ordering new planes from the US – even just to replace existing ones.

The staggering attack on the Jewish state should have provided a much-needed wake-up call to anyone who doubted that Israel is still facing an immediate existential threat from the Islamic Republic. Unfortunately, too many members of Congress needed that wake-up call. The Senate cleared a $95 billion foreign aid bill to help arm Ukraine, Israel and Taiwan in February, while the House has voted on a bill to aid only Israel.

It should be irrelevant whether the military aid for Israel is accompanied by allocations to other countries. What matters is that Israel receives the aid as soon as humanly possible.

The bills have been stalled for way too long over political technicalities. The very politically divisive Ukraine question has been particularly intrusive and counterproductive.

President Joe Biden and Senate Majority leader Chuck Schumer are at fault for conditioning aid for Israel on a completely unrelated conflict far away. Some Republicans have vowed to oppose Ukraine aid and have conditioned the aid on closing America's southern border, another issue with no relevance.

This is the time to correct those mistakes. Israel is temporarily enjoying the moral high ground for not immediately responding to the mass attack. We know too many examples from the past, including October 7, to know that it will not last very long.

Seeing how quickly Israel lost support for its war effort should persuade the Jewish state to retaliate against Iran during the short window when it still enjoys the world's backing.

Congress will also have only a short window to pass a bill that benefits Israel. All pressure should be applied to get this done one way or the other, without any further delay.

Israel fought the attack arm-in-arm with the United States and other key allies. The success in stopping each and every drone has undoubtedly brought the Israeli and American armies closer together.

After six months of fighting, the IDF is at a crossroads. It has had tremendous success in recapturing all but southern Gaza. But the goals of destroying Hamas and returning the hostages remain unachieved.

Israel is not only fighting for its people but for all of civilization, and this war is a must-win. That costs money, too.

House Speaker Mike Johnson told Fox News that he plans to move forward with Israel aid bills this week. If the bill with Ukraine cannot be passed this week, then the House should pass a standalone bill that will only require a majority if it goes through its rules committee.

It is time to pass the Israel aid bills with bipartisan support and the backing of the American Jewish establishment, and enable the much-needed money to go through.

The Jerusalem Post

Still trust Biden on Israel? Don't

Israel's people "will remain proud Jews, standing by the principles that Israel and America will continue to share long after Biden has been forgotten," the author writes.

MAY 20, 2024

For decades, religious-Zionist voters in Israel had a clear choice on Election Day.

US President Joe Biden has told his story about his conversation with Golda Meir five weeks ahead of the 1973 Yom Kippur War countless times.

Meir told the young senator from Delaware not to cast doubt on Israel's future, even in times of great peril for the Jewish state.

"Don't worry, senator," she said. "We Jews have a secret weapon in our fight: We have no place else to go."

But a different conversation with an Israeli prime minister has become more relevant since Biden's shockingly disturbing announcement to CNN last week that he would halt shipments of American weapons to Israel for the first time if Prime Minister Benjamin Netanyahu ordered a major invasion of Rafah.

At a closed-door meeting of the Senate Foreign Relations Committee in 1982, Biden warned then-prime minister Menachem Begin that military aid for Israel's war in Lebanon could be cut off. Begin responded furiously.

"Don't threaten us with cutting off aid to give up our principles," Begin said. "I'm not a Jew with trembling knees. I am a proud Jew with 3,700 years of civilized history. Nobody came to our aid when we were dying in the gas chambers and ovens. Nobody came to our aid when we were striving to create our country. We paid for it. We fought for it. We died for it. We will stand by our principles. We will defend them. And, when necessary, we will die for them again, with or without your aid."

Biden has always painted himself as pro-Israel, but it should have surprised no one that he merely carried out the threat that he issued to the Jewish state 42 years ago.

The response in Israel has been to blame Netanyahu for harming relations with the US, the IDF for not defeating Hamas fast enough, or decades of Israeli policies of outsourcing making munitions to America, in part because hey, it's free.

Don't.

The buck stops with the president of the United States, who has made a strategic decision to abandon his country's top ally at a time of its greatest need. He has insisted that Israel act only defensively even though wars are always won offensively. He has decided to try to prevent Israel from achieving its important goals of defeating Hamas, preventing further attacks from Gaza, and bringing the hostages home.

Yes, those same hostages whose families have been to the White House. The American citizens Biden spoke about as if they were family.

Biden knew he was betraying them. He knows Israel has enough armaments to defeat the final four Hamas brigades in Rafah without a new shipment, but it has a severe shortage of leverage in hostage talks with Hamas.

Whatever leverage Israel had was taken away in a couple of sentences the Arab world saw Biden utter on CNN. It's no wonder the negotiations once again ended in failure, following the sabotage.

Imagine if Biden had used that interview to threaten Qatar with becoming an international outcast instead of threatening Israel. He could have announced that if Qatar did not bring the hostages home, America would remove its military base from the country and bar American universities from having campuses in a state that sponsors terror groups like Hamas.

Biden of course would never dare do that. But he apparently could lie to Rachel Goldberg-Polin and condemn her American citizen son Hersh to languish in Gaza until his untimely demise.

Why?

Because like many politicians, Biden's ultimate loyalty is to himself and his chances of getting reelected. It used to be the Jews who were the key to victory in purple states, so he pandered to them for decades.

Now it's the Muslims in Minnesota and Michigan, the constituents of Reps. Ilhan Omar and Rashida Tlaib, who Biden mistakenly believes hold the key to his second term, and he is acting accordingly. He will now be able to tell them that while he did provide arms that killed thousands of Gazans, he could have provided even more but did not.

Biden will also allow 100,000 Palestinians to enter the United States and make other controversial decisions to reach out to those Muslim voters. The slippery slope will continue.

The tragedy of Biden's decision is that it contradicts so many statements and promises he has made for many years and even one the day before he announced the embargo.

"My commitment to the safety of the Jewish people, the security of Israel, and its right to exist as an independent Jewish state is ironclad, even when we disagree," he said at the US Holocaust Memorial on May 7. "My administration is working around the clock to free remaining hostages, just as we have freed hostages already, and we will not rest until we bring them all home." The entire audience greeted this message with thunderous applause.

In what may be an international record in speed for breaking promises, that ironclad commitment rusted in just one day.

In 2019, Judy Woodruff asked Biden on PBS NewsHour about left-wing politicians who favored cutting off aid from Israel to protest its construction over the pre-1967 border.

"That would be a tragic mistake," he said. "The idea that we would cut off military aid to an ally, our only true, true ally in the entire region, is absolutely preposterous. It's just beyond my comprehension why anyone would do that."

Preposterous as it may be, Biden was criticizing himself five years later. His actions will be remembered, not his words.

This is a critical juncture in Israel's existential war to defeat Hamas. Israel will win this war, with or without Biden.

Its people do not have trembling knees. They will remain proud Jews, standing by the principles that Israel and America will continue to share long after Biden has been forgotten.

The Jerusalem Post

When diplomacy fails: It's time for Israel to bomb and invade Lebanon

Israel has been fighting with its hands behind its back throughout this war. Reliant on the US for munitions, the Jewish state has accepted one improper demand after another from Washington.

JUNE 23, 2024

Even though I am a frequent critic of US President Joe Biden's handling of Israel, I truly hope and pray that he will succeed in ending the current war with victory for the Jewish state in Gaza and in preventing an escalation in Lebanon.

His envoy, Amos Hochstein, expressed confidence in Beirut on Tuesday that a diplomatic solution could be found to end the conflict.

"The conflict along the Blue Line between Israel and Hezbollah has gone on for long enough," Hochstein said. "Innocent people are dying. Property is damaged. Families are shattered, and the Lebanese economy continues to decline. The country is suffering for no good reason. It's in everyone's interest to resolve it quickly and diplomatically. That is both achievable and urgent."

But allow me to be skeptical of the chances of success via the diplomatic route, due to the maniacal antisemitism of Hamas, Hezbollah, and their Iranian benefactors, and the ineptitude of the Biden administration on Israel.

Any agreement would require Hezbollah to keep its commitments under UN Resolution 1701 to disarm completely and leave the area south of the Litani River, and no one believes that, after 18 years, they will suddenly honor their commitments. That resolution ended the Second Lebanon War, and since then, Hezbollah has amassed more than 150,000 rockets and become the dominant force in the Lebanese government.

So all that's left is the military approach.

That, too, has been tried you say?

Not really. Israel has been fighting with its hands behind its back throughout this war. Reliant on the US for munitions, the Jewish state has accepted one improper demand after another from Washington.

The time has come for a much more aggressive approach in both Gaza and in Lebanon. Israel should immediately bomb deep into Lebanon and invade its northern neighbor.

There are three key reasons: Too many Israelis have been displaced for too long; there is no way to win the war without smashing our enemies; and our approach in Gaza has failed, resulting in lessons that must be learned immediately.

The 60,000 evacuees from northern communities left their homes on October 7 expecting to be back after several days. It has already been several months – eight and a half, to be exact – and their plight has been ignored by both Israeli officials and the wider world.

Even educated news consumers in America do not know that more rockets have been fired at Israel in this war from Lebanon than from Gaza and that 80 square kilometers (31 sq. miles) have been engulfed in flames.

There are also too many Israelis living in fear in areas that were not evacuated but have been reached by Hezbollah rockets in this war. We have been putting our children's lives in jeopardy, and the time has come for that to stop.

I have supported Prime Minister Benjamin Netanyahu and his right-wing coalition. But there is no point in keeping the government together if it cannot perform its minimal obligation of keeping its residents and citizens safe.

The government owes its northern residents to fight in a way that will be more effective. Wars are not won defensively or with a sanitized approach on offense.

The second reason for invading Lebanon: We must fight to win.

Israel has been bragging to the world about its relative success in minimizing its enemy's casualties in urban warfare – certainly when compared to the United States. That success has come at the unacceptable cost of the lives of our young soldiers who were prohibited from opening fire.

I am all for setting rules. But rules are meant to be broken when it comes to minimizing IDF casualties and saving the lives of our boys and girls in a war against evil.

The time has come for Israel to use full force and to stop worrying about how America will respond. Israel has to set its own policies; if they meet bipartisan US standards, great, but if they do not, so be it.

The idea that the IDF has to run a sanitized Supreme Court-approved war needs to be thrown out. That might work well for skirmishes or for small operations, but it simply doesn't work in a serious, multi-front war.

Of course, there will be many casualties on our side if we invade Lebanon, but the IDF will take the necessary precautions to keep its soldiers protected, and the only way you win is by inflicting tremendous losses on your enemy. There is a need to destroy and kill: That is what war is about.

That brings us to the final reason to escalate war in Lebanon: We are losing the war in Gaza, because we have been overly cautious. Too much effort is being made to provide humanitarian aid to an enemy population in Gaza, who instead of providing information to help us find our hostages have been holding them captive themselves.

That was another improper demand of the Biden administration, which is withholding a key shipment of 2,000-pound bombs that could be used for the kind of strikes that could end the war successfully.

When Netanyahu comes to Congress next month, he will surely claim victory in the war. I hope by then he will be justified in doing so.

For now, saying it would be absurd. Rockets fired from Gaza over Tel Aviv and as far north as near Ra'anana (almost 90 km.) eight months into a war is not a sign of winning.

It is a sign of insanity.

After decades of quoting Albert Einstein saying "the definition of insanity is doing the same thing over and over again and expecting different results," it turns out he never said that.

The Ultimate Quotable Einstein, an authoritative complication of his most memorable utterances, identified the quote as a misattribution.

Here is a quote that he did say: "I think and think for months and years. Ninety-nine times, the conclusion is false. The hundredth time, I am right."

Israel is no genius like Einstein and cannot afford to be wrong again. This is the time to bomb and invade Lebanon – and to finally get it right.

The Jerusalem Post

A great existential threat: A Harris presidency's impact on Israel

Had Harris attended Netanyahu's speech, or at least taken a few minutes to read it, perhaps she would have realized that her words were wrong, and silence would have been a much better choice.

AUGUST 11, 2024

On July 25, I had the honor and privilege of attending Prime Minister Benjamin Netanyahu's spectacular speech to Congress. He beautifully articulated the tremendous threats Israel is facing, the historical connection of the Jewish people to the Land of Israel, the sensitivity of the current situation, and how far Israel goes to prevent harm to civilians – beyond what any army has ever done in history.

The unprecedented applause Netanyahu received from both sides of the aisle as he articulated his vision emboldened Israel against its enemies and could have gone a long way toward ending the war with the best possible outcome for Israel's future security. Except there was one problem. I was at the speech, but I am not the vice president of the United States and the current front-runner for the presidency. And the woman who is made a point of not being there.

Vice President Kamala Harris should have been sitting on the dais behind Netanyahu at Congress that day to demonstrate her commitment to America's top ally. But more importantly, she ought to have been there to listen to one of the world's elder statesmen and learn from him.

Her decision to go, instead, to a sorority sent a message to Israel's enemies that if she got elected, God forbid, they could do whatever they wanted to the Jewish state, and she would look the other way.

Just in case Iran and its proxies did not get that message, she sharpened it following her meeting with Netanyahu, when in a completely unnecessary and frightening address to the public, she described her conversation with the prime minister of Israel as "frank."

"I also expressed with the prime minister my serious concern about the scale of human suffering in Gaza, including the death of far too many innocent civilians," she said in an accusatory tone. "And I made clear my serious concern about the dire humanitarian situation there, with over two million people facing high levels of food insecurity and half a million people facing catastrophic levels of acute food insecurity."

Was Harris aware that while she spoke, there were hundreds of trucks of food and aid waiting on the Gazan side of the border that Israel let in, but the UN was not delivering? Did she not know that it was Hamas and the UN that deserved her scolding?

"What has happened in Gaza over the past nine months is devastating – the images of dead children and desperate, hungry people fleeing for safety, something was appointed by former US president Donald Trump and were displaced for the second, third, or fourth time," she said, lecturing and shaming America's ally. "We cannot look away in the face of these tragedies. We cannot allow ourselves to become numb to the suffering. And I will not be silent."

Had Harris attended Netanyahu's speech, or at least taken a few minutes to read it, perhaps she would have realized that her words were wrong, and silence would have been a much better choice.

I want to commend the editor-in-chief of The Jerusalem Post, Zvika Klein, for taking a bold stand against a potential Harris presidency in his most recent, well-articulated, Friday column, and American voters who read the Post should realize the importance of his message.

"Harris as president could be a disaster for Israel and the Jewish people," was his headline on Jpost.com. Yet, Klein did not go far enough. A Harris presidency not only 'could be a disaster for Israel and the Jewish people,' it would be the greatest existential threat Israel has ever faced.

American voters need to wake up and realize that Kamala Harris is a dangerous radical who wants the United States as we know it brought down. Her sympathy is not with Israel but with the people of Gaza, who invaded Israel on October 7, murdered 1,200 people, kidnapped more than 250, and raped numerous people of all ages.

Kamala's victory would persuade Iran to escalate its nuclear weapons program, its proxies to intensify their rocket fire, and Qatar to continue harboring terrorists.

The Democratic Party has replaced President Joe Biden as its presidential candidate with a woman who is to the Left of Bernie Sanders. She then added insult to injury by picking progressive running mate Tim Walz to push the ticket even further leftward while rejecting Josh Shapiro, the pro-Israel Jewish governor of the key state of Pennsylvania – which could decide the election in November. She gave in to the Squad with that choice, and she would let them decide her Middle East policy if she were elected.

Living in a democracy gives you the freedom to vote on a lot of issues that are important to you. Perhaps, if these were less sensitive times, or if there was a candidate such as Biden, with decades of calling himself pro-Israel, Jewish voters could afford to cast their ballots based on their views on abortion or the environment.

But now Israel is in the middle of a seven-front war, the world is fraught with danger, and the Democratic candidate for president is a foreign affairs novice whose views on Israel are downright scary.

Voters need to keep in mind that they will be selecting the leader of the free world, not just someone they might want to spend time with.

Presidential candidate Donald Trump has been the best US president for Israel, and voters know he can be trusted to keep both America and Israel safe. He owes it to the world to win and to stop being his own worst enemy.

Harris and Walz, by contrast, have no advantages, and letting her take over the White House would make America less safe and put Israel in great peril.

We have seen what happens when American Jews set aside their differences and unite to defeat anti-Israel candidates. Synagogues in New York that have barred politics from the pulpit for decades permitted weekly addresses against Jamal Bowman until he lost. And the diverse Jewish community of St Louis joined together last week to force out antisemitic congresswoman Cori Bush.

The time has come to do what worked in New York and St Louis on a national level in order to ensure Harris's defeat and send a message that being anti-Israel is not an electoral asset. Harris must be beaten so handily that no party will ever again field a candidate who is not a strong supporter of the Jewish state.

Then, the next time Netanyahu or another Israeli prime minister comes to Washington, the future leaders of the US will be there as they should be, listening and applauding.

The Jewish Press

How Pro-Israel Americans Could Keep Kamala From Becoming President

SEPTEMBER 19, 2024

"Elana" is an 18-year-old Freshman at Vanderbilt who was raised in West Bloomfield, Michigan in a family that cares deeply about the fate of Israel.

She has never expressed any interest in politics, but she could decide one of America's most fateful elections ever and prevent Israel from great danger.

It is not too late for "Elana" and others like her to get the ballots that could ensure that Donald Trump returns to the White House and Kamala Harris will never get there. But they must take immediate action.

The 2000 presidential race was decided by 537 absentee ballots cast in Florida. Polls indicate that the current election could be just as close, so every vote in swing states is crucial.

"Elana" could end up casting the deciding vote.

Now for why that matters. I watched last Tuesday night's presidential debate, and I agree with Donald Trump.

"If she's president, I believe that Israel will not exist within two years from now," he said. "And I've been pretty good at predictions. And I hope I'm wrong about that one. She hates Israel."

Harris made faces when he said that. But her words proved him right.

"Far too many innocent Palestinians have been killed," she said. "Children, mothers. What we know is that this war must end. It must end immediately, and the way it will end is we need a cease-fire deal, and we need the hostages out. And so we will continue to work around the clock on that."

Immediately? How about letting Israel and its democratically elected government decide when it has completed the goals of this war, which include destroying Hamas and preventing it from being able to rule Gaza or attack Israel ever again?

And why did she not blame the terrorist organization for the deaths of both Israelis and Palestinians in this war? Or how about correcting biased mediator Linsey Davis, who quoted Hamas statistics as if they were Gospel?

Harris did not stop there in her patronizing criticism of Israel and its people. She professed moral equivalence as her doctrine when true morality is needed more than ever in the Middle East.

"We must chart a course for a two-state solution," she said. "And in that solution, there must be security for the Israeli people and Israel – and in equal measure for the Palestinians."

News flash for Kamala: Polls over the last few years have found that a majority of Israelis no longer back creating a hostile terror state in their biblical heartland. And polls of Palestinians have never found a majority of them favored letting Israel exist.

That was all before October 7. After the Palestinians murdered 1200 Israelis in one day, she has a lot of chutzpah to tell America's closest ally that she cares about the security of their murderers "in equal measure."

If Harris becomes president, residents of northern Israel will be in great danger. She will not recognize Israeli sovereignty over the Golan like Trump did as president, nor will she utter a half-persuasive "don't" to Hizbullah like President Biden. Hizbullah will have a field day and get away every day with murder.

Harris will neither project strength, nor use it. She says she will let Israel defend itself but she is obsessed with how.

That how is with defensive measures. But defensive measures cannot win a war that must be won.

Trump, by contrast, presented a clear vision for the Middle East in the debate. He proved once again that he, unlike Harris, knows who the bad guys are.

"Iran was broke under Donald Trump," he said. "Now Iran has $300 billion because they took off all the sanctions that I had. Iran had no money for Hamas or Hezbollah or any of the 28 different spheres of terror. And they are spheres of terror. Horrible terror. They had no money. It was a big story, and you know it. You covered it. Very well, actually. They had no money for terror. They were broke. Now they're a rich nation. And now what they're doing is spreading that money around. Look at what's happening with the Houthis and Yemen. Look at what's going on in the Middle East. This would have never happened. I will get that settled and fast."

While confused American Jews continue to vote overwhelmingly for Democratic candidates, in Israel it is the opposite. Israelis know what Trump did for them as president, and they greatly appreciate it.

The junction in front of the American embassy in Jerusalem that he finally moved to Israel's eternal capital is named Donald Trump Square. That was a campaign promise, and unlike his predecessors who made similar promises, he kept it, and I attended the ceremony unveiling the embassy.

Israelis also see through Kamala Harris, who boycotted their prime minister's brilliant speech to Congress that I attended and she did not.

Harris will appoint apologists and even allies of Iran to key positions of power. She will project weakness, and all Iranian proxies will be emboldened, which could make the security problems in Israel spiral out of control.

When Iran gets a nuclear bomb and casts a nuclear shadow over the Middle East, what will she do? Make another face? Laugh another laugh?

The continued existence of the world's only Jewish state is no laughing matter.

This is why "Elana" and Americans of all ages who care about Israel must take steps to vote right away.

The future of Israel's nearly 10 million residents depends on it.

The Israel National News

How Israelis Could Keep Kamala From Killing Them

SEPTEMBER 20, 2024

"Eliana" is an 18-year-old resident of northern Israel born to a mother who made Aliyah from West Bloomfield, Michigan.

She has never lived in the United States or expressed any interest in politics, but she could decide one of America's most fateful elections ever and prevent Israel from great danger.

It is not too late for "Eliana" and others like her to get the ballots that could ensure that Donald Trump returns to the White House and Kamala Harris will never get there. But they must take immediate action.
First, here are the facts:

American citizens who have made aliyah and are dual citizens have the right to vote in US elections. Children of American citizens born abroad who have never resided in the US can vote in 18 States. The only potential swing states among the 18 are Michigan, Arizona, Georgia and Wisconsin.

There are an estimated 200,000 eligible American voters in Israel, and in recent elections, Israelis voted more than residents of any other foreign country.

How many of them are from those four states? Several thousand- mostly from Atlanta, Phoenix, Milwaukee and Detroit.

That may not sound like much, but the 2000 presidential race was decided by 537 absentee ballots cast in Florida, of which only 64 came from Israel.

"Eliana" could end up casting the deciding vote.

Now for why that matters. I watched Tuesday night's presidential debate, and I agree with Donald Trump.

"If she's president, I believe that Israel will not exist within two years from now," he said. "And I've been pretty good at predictions. And I hope I'm wrong about that one. She hates Israel."

Harris made faces when he said that. But her words proved him right. "Far too many innocent Palestinians have been killed," she said.

"Children, mothers. What we know is that this war must end. It must end immediately, and the way it will end is we need a cease-fire deal, and we need the hostages out. And so we will continue to work around the clock on that."

Immediately? How about letting Israel and its democratically elected government decide when it has completed the goals of this war, which include destroying Hamas and preventing it from being able to rule Gaza or attack Israel ever again?

And why did she not blame the terrorist organization for the deaths of both Israelis and Palestinians in this war? Or how about correcting biased mediator Linsey Davis, who quoted Hamas statistics as if they were Gospel?

Harris did not stop there in her patronizing criticism of Israel and its people. She professed moral equivalence as her doctrine when true morality is needed more than ever in the Middle East.

"We must chart a course for a two-state solution," she said. "And in that solution, there must be security for the Israeli people and Israel – and in equal measure for the Palestinians."

News flash for Kamala: Polls over the last few years have found that a majority of Israelis no longer back creating a hostile terror state in their biblical heartland. And polls of Palestinians have never found a majority of them favored letting Israel exist.

That was all before October 7. After the Palestinians murdered 1200 Israelis in one day, she has a lot of chutzpah to tell America's closest ally that she cares about the security of their murderers "in equal measure."

If Harris becomes president, residents of northern Israel like "Eliana" will be in great danger. She will not recognize Israeli sovereignty over the Golan like Trump did as president, nor will she utter a half-persuasive "don't" to Hizbullah like President Biden. Hizbullah will have a field day and get away every day with murder.

Harris will neither project strength, nor use it. She says she will let Israel defend itself but she is obsessed with how.

That how is with defensive measures. But defensive measures cannot win a war that must be won.

Trump, by contrast, presented a clear vision for the Middle East in the debate. He proved once again that he, unlike Harris, knows who the bad guys are.

"Iran was broke under Donald Trump," he said. "Now Iran has $300 billion because they took off all the sanctions that I had. Iran had no money for Hamas or Hezbollah or any of the 28 different spheres of terror. And they are spheres of terror. Horrible terror. They had no money. It was a big story, and you know it. You covered it. Very well, actually. They had no money for terror. They were broke. Now they're a rich nation. And now what they're doing is spreading that money around. Look at what's happening with the Houthis and Yemen. Look at what's going on in the Middle East. This would have never happened. I will get that settled and fast."

While confused American Jews continue to vote overwhelmingly for Democratic candidates, in Israel it is the opposite. Israelis know what Trump did for them as president, and they greatly appreciate it.

The junction in front of the American embassy in Jerusalem that he finally moved to Israel's eternal capital is named Donald Trump Square. That was a campaign promise, and unlike his predecessors who made similar promises, he kept it, and I attended the ceremony unveiling the embassy.

Israelis also see through Kamala Harris, who boycotted their prime minister's brilliant speech to Congress that I attended and she did not.

Harris will appoint apologists and even allies of Iran to key positions of power. She will project weakness, and all Iranian proxies will be emboldened, which could make the security problems in Israel spiral out of control.

When Iran gets a nuclear bomb and casts a nuclear shadow over the Middle East, what will she do? Make another face? Laugh another laugh?

The continued existence of the world's only Jewish state is no laughing matter.

This is why Americans living in Israel and their children must take steps to vote right away. They can go to IvoteIsrael.com, which simplifies the process.

The future of "Eliana" and nearly 10 million other Israelis depends on it.

Index

The Algemeiner, 91, 112, 147, 161

Abraham Accords, 151, 153-154, 172, 190-195, 197, 200, 207, 212, 221

antisemitism, 19-22, 44, 75-77, 79, 98, 102, 144-146, 150, 157, 159, 185-186, 196, 208-210, 212-214, 216, 218-222, 235, 242

Benny Gantz, 82, 100, 104, 110, 112, 121, 131, 141, 199, 203, 226

Biden, 126, 131-132, 141-142, 145-146, 149-154, 168, 170, 172, 182-184, 191-193, 195, 197-201, 203, 205-207, 224-225, 229, 231-235, 238, 241, 244, 249

COVID, 2-3, 120, 128, 133, 135, 142, 156, 163

David Friedman, 30, 33, 59, 88, 111, 129

Democrat, 11, 24, 27, 40-41, 72, 75-76, 79, 97-98, 116-117, 121, 123, 126, 133, 141, 143, 151-152, 154, 182, 185, 193, 223, 241, 245, 249

Hamas, 35-36, 48-50, 53, 88, 93, 144, 161, 170, 172, 182, 188, 205-213, 219-220, 224-225, 229, 232, 234-235, 240, 244-245, 248-249

Ilhan Omar, 75, 97, 133, 185-186, 200, 233

Iran, 8-9, 24, 35-38, 40-41, 49-50, 52-54, 58-59, 82, 88, 92, 94, 108, 121, 130-132, 134, 142, 149, 168-170, 183, 191-193, 195, 206, 210, 212, 222, 228-229, 240-241, 245-246, 249-250

Israel National News, 118, 194, 216, 247

The Jerusalem Post, 8, 19, 26, 29, 35, 37, 40, 43, 45, 48, 532, 55, 58, 61, 63, 66, 72, 75, 78, 81, 84, 87, 94, 97, 99, 102, 105, 108, 115, 120, 123, 127, 131, 134, 138, 141, 144, 150, 153, 156, 159, 164, 168, 171, 178, 182, 185, 188, 191, 197, 202, 205, 211, 218, 223, 228, 231, 235, 239

The Jewish Home, 174

The Jewish Press, 5, 12, 16, 23, 32, 69, 153, 243

Mizrachi, 61, 70, 138-140, 164-167, 178-180

Naftali Bennett, 61, 65, 103, 147, 150, 153, 161, 164-165, 169, 175, 180

Netanyahu, 14, 20, 23-24, 46, 52-53, 59, 61, 63, 65, 68, 72-73, 81-82, 84, 97-98, 100, 103, 110, 112, 115-129, 131, 141, 143, 147-148, 159-161, 169, 173-174, 176, 180, 182-184, 188-191, 193, 197-198, 200-205, 208, 222-223, 225-227, 231-232, 236, 238-240, 242

Obama, 8, 19-23, 29, 32, 39, 53, 81, 94, 106, 110, 112-113, 126, 131-132, 134, 183, 193

Palestine, 20-22, 36, 40-41, 48, 50, 65, 85, 89, 95-97, 105-106, 109-110, 113, 115-118, 124-126, 128-129, 144-145, 150-151, 153-154, 171-173, 179, 189, 197-201, 206-207, 217, 220, 233, 243-244, 248-249

Qatar, 35-36, 48-50, 129, 188-190, 210-211, 213, 220-221, 232, 241

Religious Zionists of America, 27, 70, 118, 140, 165, 194

Saudi Arabia, 35, 37-39, 48-49, 54, 57, 92, 113, 129, 151, 154, 172, 189, 191, 198-201, 206-207, 210

Smotrich, 178-183, 199-200, 204

Trump, 19, 22, 24, 29-35, 37, 41, 43-44, 49, 52-54, 58-60, 78-79, 82, 87-88, 92, 94-96, 98, 103, 106, 108, 110, 112-117, 120, 123-136, 141-143, 145, 151, 153-154, 170, 172, 185, 197-198, 220, 240-241

UAE, 35, 48-50, 127-130, 134, 142, 170, 191-193, 195, 197, 221, 243-245, 247-249

United Nations, 21, 23, 28, 35, 46, 52, 62, 67, 82, 88, 108, 130-132, 145, 195, 203, 216, 218, 235, 240

West Bank, 21, 89, 105, 125, 172, 198, 207

World Zionist Organization, 5, 61, 138, 165

Yair Lapid, 82, 141, 147, 149-150, 153, 157, 161, 199

Made in the USA
Middletown, DE
17 October 2024